Thema 1 Ich persönlich

A The present tense

STUDENT BOOK 1.1 | GRAMMAR SECTION F1

The present tense is used to talk about what is happening now, or what happens regularly. Weak (regular) verbs follow the same pattern as *wohnen* (to live). Take the *-en* off the infinitive to give the stem (*wohn-*). Add the endings shown below.

wohnen			
ich	wohn**e**	wir	wohn**en**
du	wohn**st**	ihr	wohn**t**
er/sie/es/man	wohn**t**	Sie/sie	wohn**en**

Note: if the stem of the verb ends in a *-t* or a *-d*, add an *-e* in the second person familiar, singular and plural, and third person singular, e.g. *er arbeitet*.

1 Rewrite these sentences with the correct form of the verb in brackets in the present tense.
e.g. Er (*spielen*) gern Fußball. → Er **spielt** gern Fußball.

a Wir (*hören*) Musik.
Wir hören Musik

b Was (*machen*) ihr?
Was macht ihr?

c Der Junge (*sagen*), er heißt Karl.
Der Junge sagt, er heißt Karl

d (*Wohnen*) du in Hamburg?
Wohnst du in Hamburg?

e Meine Mutter (*arbeiten*) heute.
Meine Mutter arbeitet heute

f Was (*bedeuten*) das?
Was bedeutet das?

g Meine Großeltern (*reisen*) nach Spanien.
Meine Großeltern reisen nach Spanien

h Ihr (*spielen*) Tennis nach der Schule.
Ihr spielt Tennis nach der Schule

i Ich (*arbeiten*) am Wochenende.
Ich arbeite am Wochenende

j Sabine (*besuchen*) ihre Schwester.
Sabine besucht ihre Schwester

k (*Bauen*) ihr ein neues Haus?
Baut ihr ein neues Haus?

Strong (irregular) ... of the tenses, but ... there is a vowel c... *es/man* forms, as ...

A very important strong verb is *sein* (to be). Make sure you learn it.

Some verbs are a mixture of strong and weak. They have the same endings as weak verbs, but are irregular in other ways. An important mixed verb is *haben*.

haben			
ich	habe	wir	haben
du	hast	ihr	habt
er/sie/es/man	hat	Sie/sie	haben

sehen			
ich	sehe	wir	sehen
du	siehst	ihr	seht
er/sie/es/man	sieht	Sie/sie	sehen

fahren			
ich	fahre	wir	fahren
du	fährst	ihr	fahrt
er/sie/es/man	fährt	Sie/sie	fahren

2 All the following verbs are strong or mixed. Use the verb tables at the back to look up and write in the *er/sie/es/man* form in the present tense. You will find this in the second column in the tables. Add the English meaning of the infinitive. The first one has been done for you.

Infinitive	Third person present	English
essen	isst	to eat
gehen	geht	to go
sprechen	spricht	to speak
wissen	wisst	to know
denken	denkt	to think
lesen	lisst	to read
geben	gibt	to give
schreiben	schribt	to write
trinken	trinkt	to drink

3 Use the information above to work out how to translate the following:
e.g. I read → **Ich lese**

a They speak ....
b You (familiar, s) write ....

c We give ....
d She has ....
e You (polite) eat ....
f I drink ....
g They are ....
h You (familiar, pl) read ....
i He goes ....
j The children think ....
k They know ....
l The man eats ....
m You (familiar, s) speak ....

B Coordinating conjunctions

STUDENT BOOK 1.1 **GRAMMAR SECTION H3**

> **Conjunctions** link two parts of a sentence. The coordinating conjunctions *und* (and), *aber* (but) and *oder* (or) do not require a change in the word order.
>
> Ich heiße Maria **und** ich wohne in Köln.
>
> Er hat eine Schwester **aber** er hat keinen Bruder.
>
> Other coordinating conjunctions are:
>
> *entweder...oder* (either...or), *denn* (because, as), *sondern* (but: used after a negative)
>
> Ich wohne nicht in München, **sondern** in Düsseldorf.

4 Choose a conjunction from the box to fill in each gap in this dialogue. The first gap has been filled for you.

> und   ~~oder~~   denn
> aber   entweder   sondern

A Hallo. Kommst du aus Spanien **oder** Italien?

B Nein, ich komme nicht aus Europa, ... aus Südamerika.

A Wie interessant! Wie alt bist du?

B Ich bin fünfzehn Jahre alt .... ich werde morgen sechzehn.

A Alles Gute zum Geburtstag. Was bekommst du als Geschenk?

B .... einen neuen Computer oder einen Fernseher.

A Toll! Ich bin auch fünfzehn .... ich habe am 6. Mai Geburtstag.

B OK. Ich muss jetzt gehen, ... mein Bus fährt gleich ab. Tschüs!

C Plural nouns

STUDENT BOOK 1.2 **GRAMMAR SECTION A2**

> In German there are lots of different ways to form plurals. Below are some of the most common forms.
>
> **Masculine** nouns often show their plural by adding an -e and/or placing an umlaut over one of the vowels:
>
> der Bruder → die Br**ü**der
>
> der Großvater → die Großv**ä**ter
>
> **Feminine** nouns often add -n or -en:
>
> die Schwester → die Schwester**n**
>
> **Neuter** nouns often add -e or -er:
>
> das Kind → die Kind**er**
>
> When you learn a new noun, you should learn its plural at the same time. This information will always be given in a dictionary or glossary.

5 These singular nouns appear as in a glossary. Write them out fully in their plural form.

Singular	Plural
der Onkel (-)	**die Onkel**
die Tante (-n)	
die Tochter (¨)	
der Bruder (¨)	
das Kind (-er)	
der Mann (¨er)	
die Frau (-en)	
die Familie (-n)	
der Teenager (-)	
die Schwester (-n)	
der Sohn (¨e)	
die Mutter (¨)	
der Großvater (¨)	

6 Use the information in this family tree and words from the list above to complete the gaps in the text about Jonas's family. The first gap has been filled for you.

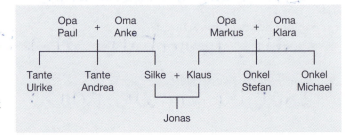

Ich heiße Jonas. Ich habe zwei **Großväter**, Paul und Markus. Ich habe auch zwei G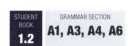............, Anke und Klara. Opa Paul und Oma Anke haben drei T.............................. Meine Mutter, Silke, hat zwei S..............................., Ulrike und Andrea. Sie sind meine T............................... Opa Markus und Oma Klara haben drei S............................... Also habe ich zwei O............................... Ich bin Einzelkind. Ich habe keine S............................... und keine B...............................

D Gender, case and definite and indefinite articles

STUDENT BOOK 1.2 — GRAMMAR SECTION A1, A3, A4, A6

All German nouns are either masculine (*der*), feminine (*die*) or neuter (*das*). *Der*, *die* and *das* are the definite articles (the). In the plural the definite article is *die* for nouns of all three genders. The indefinite article (a, an) is *ein* (m), *eine* (f), *ein* (n).

All German nouns also have a case. The cases are called: nominative, accusative, genitive and dative. If the noun is the subject of the sentence, it is in the nominative case. If it is the object of the sentence, it is in the accusative case.

Definite article

	m	f	n	pl
Nom	der	die	das	die
Acc	den	die	das	die
Gen	des	der	des	der
Dat	dem	der	dem	den

Indefinite article

	m	f	n
Nom	ein	eine	ein
Acc	einen	eine	ein
Gen	eines	einer	eines
Dat	einem	einer	einem

7 It is important that you can identify the subject and object so that you know whether to use the nominative or accusative. In each sentence, put a ring around the subject and underline the object.

e.g. (The man) is eating <u>a banana</u>.

a I speak German.
b The children are wearing pyjamas.
c She is visiting the town.
d My uncle likes chocolate.
e Do you have a pen?
f The boy asks a question.
g We love sport.
h Someone I know.
i They don't have children.
j My grandfather smokes a pipe.
k He loves her.
l Everything we do.

8 Insert the correct form of the definite article in the gaps. Decide whether the noun is being used in the nominative or accusative (is it the subject or the object?) and then make sure you know if it is masculine, feminine, neuter or plural so that you can choose the correct article from the table.

e.g. Ich mag.................... Katze. → Ich mag **die** Katze.

a .... Frau arbeitet in der Stadtmitte.
b Mein Bruder sieht.................... Bus.
c .... Haus ist groß.
d .... Junge ist vierzehn Jahre alt.
e Ich finde.................... Kinder nett.
f Kennst du.................... Mann?
g .... Zwillingsbrüder sind lustig.

9 Insert the correct form of the indefinite article in each gap, taking into account the gender of the noun and whether it is being used in the nominative or accusative case.

e.g. Ich habe.................... Schwester. → Ich habe **eine** Schwester.

a .... Mann wohnt hier.
b Wir haben.................... Stiefmutter.
c Meine Kusine hat.................... Kind.
d .... Mädchen singt.
e .... Lehrer arbeitet in einer Schule.
f Das Baby ist.................... Jahr alt.
g Haben Sie.................... Stiefsohn?

E Possessive adjectives

Possessive adjectives are words like 'my', 'your', 'his', 'her' etc. Their gender and number (s or pl) must agree with the noun they refer to. They also have different endings in different cases. The endings are the same as for the indefinite article, as shown in the table below using the example *sein* (his). The other possessive adjectives are:

my	mein
your (informal singular)	dein
his	sein
her	ihr
its	sein
our	unser
your (informal plural)	euer
their	ihr
your (formal)	Ihr

	m	f	n	pl
Nom	sein	seine	sein	seine
Acc	seinen	seine	sein	seine
Gen	seines	seiner	seines	seiner
Dat	seinem	seiner	seinem	seinen

10 Match up the German and English. One example has been done for you, as shown by the arrow.

a deine Mutter
b Ihr Großvater
c unser Kind
d mein Zwillingsbruder
e euer Vater
f ihre Eltern
g sein Kind
h ihre Mutter
i eure Eltern
j mein Großvater

i his child
ii her parents
iii your mother
iv my grandfather
v her mother
vi your grandfather
vii your parents
viii my twin brother
ix our child
x your father

F Quantifiers

Quantifiers are combined with adjectives to give a more precise idea of amount or extent:

Er ist alt. He is old.

*Er ist **sehr** alt*. He is **very** old.

These words are adverbs and so never have an ending. Some other quantifiers are: *ziemlich* (quite), *extrem* (extremely), *ein bisschen* (a little), *etwas* (somewhat).

11 Choose qualifiers and adjectives from the box to end these sentences so that they match the English.

frech	~~sehr~~	extrem	ziemlich
geduldig	sehr	ehrlich	~~sympathisch~~
ein bisschen	launisch	etwas	faul

e.g. Unsere Oma ist........................ ....
(very nice) → Unsere Oma ist **sehr sympathisch**.

a Mein Vater ist........................ ....
(extremely patient)

b Deine Schwester ist........................ ....
(quite moody)

c Ihr Freund ist........................ ....
(somewhat lazy)

d Sein Onkel ist........................ ....
(very honest)

e Du bist........................ ....
(a bit cheeky)

Thema 2 Mein Zuhause

A Adjectives

STUDENT BOOK 2.1 | **GRAMMAR SECTION B1–B3**

Adjectives are used to describe nouns, e.g. *groß* (big), *schön* (nice). If they come after a noun they do not need an ending and are used in the form which you would find if you looked up the words in a dictionary, e.g.

*Das Haus ist **groß**.*

*Der Garten ist **schön**.*

If, however, you place an adjective in front of the noun, it will need an ending. The ending will change according to the gender of the noun, whether the noun is singular or plural, which case is being used and whether the adjective follows the definite article, the indefinite article, or no article at all. The table shows how the endings change in the nominative and accusative. Note: the articles and the endings are in bold type so that you can see how they change.

Definite article (the)		m	f	n	pl
Nom	Das ist/ sind…	**der** groß**e** Garten	**die** groß**e** Küche	**das** groß**e** Haus	**die** groß**en** Häuser
Acc	Ich mag…	**den** groß**en** Garten	**die** groß**e** Küche	**das** groß**e** Haus	**die** groß**en** Häuser

Indefinite article (a, an, some)		m	f	n	pl
Nom	Das ist/ sind…	**ein** groß**er** Garten	**eine** groß**e** Küche	**ein** groß**es** Haus	groß**e** Häuser
Acc	Ich mag…	**einen** groß**en** Garten	**eine** groß**e** Küche	**ein** groß**es** Haus	groß**e** Häuser

1 Look carefully at the table and answer these questions.

a Which genders keep the same adjective ending in the accusative as in the nominative?

....

b Which gender has the same adjective ending after both the definite and indefinite article in the accusative, but not in the nominative?

....

c Why is there no article before the plural adjectives in the indefinite article table?

....

d Look at the nominative row for the indefinite article. The indefinite article (*ein*) is the same for both masculine and neuter, but the adjectives have different endings. Can you think of a way to remember that the masculine is *-er* and the neuter is *-es*?

....
....

2 Identify the adjective in each sentence. Copy it into the first column of the first row and put ✓ or ✗ in the second column to show if it has an ending or not. If it has, continue to fill in the boxes to show whether it follows a definite or indefinite article and which gender and case are used. The first one has been done for you:

	Adjective	Ending?	Definite article	Indefinite article	m	f	n	pl	Nom	Acc
a	neue	✓		✓	✓					✓
b										
c										
d										
e										
f										
g										
h										
i										
j										

a Das Haus hat eine neue Garage.

b Unsere Wohnung ist ziemlich klein.

c Hier ist das moderne Reihenhaus.

d Wir haben ein gemütliches Wohnzimmer.

e Die Küche ist sehr altmodisch.

f Im Garten sehen Sie große Bäume.

g Peters Wohnung hat einen engen Balkon.

h Junge Menschen wohnen in diesem Studentenwohnheim.

i Ein schöner Garten liegt hinter dem Einfamilienhaus.

j Siehst du die neuen Hochhäuser?

3 Read this description of a house and add the correct endings. You may need to leave some gaps blank if an ending is not required. The first gap has been filled in for you.

Wir haben ein alt**es** Reihenhaus. Ich habe ein klein…….. Schlafzimmer aber das Wohnzimmer ist riesig …….. Es gibt eine neu……. Küche und auch ein modern……. Büro, wo meine Mutter arbeitet. Leider haben wir nur einen klein……. Garten, aber direkt gegenüber liegt ein schön……. Park, wo ich mit meinen Freunden spielen kann. Dort gibt es groß…….. Bäume, bunt……. Blumen und einen lustig……. Kinderspielplatz. Die Kinder im Park sind meistens sehr freundlich……..

B Adverbs

> Adverbs and adjectives are often the same in German, whereas English adverbs often have '-ly' on the end. If you see a word that could be an adverb or an adjective and has no ending, check whether it is describing a noun or a verb to work out which it is.
>
> Das **Auto** ist **langsam**.
>
> The car is slow.
> (adjective describing the noun)
>
> Meine Mutter **fährt langsam**.
>
> My mother drives slowly.
> (adverb describing the verb)

4 Translate these sentences into English. For each one, say whether it contains an adjective or adverb.

e.g. Dieses Einfamilienhaus ist toll für deine Familie. → This detached house is great for your family. (adjective)

a Wir wohnen glücklich in der Stadtmitte.

....

....

....

b Alle Menschen in dieser Siedlung sind alt.

....

....

....

c Hier sind die Häuser nicht so teuer.

....

....

....

d Mit der S-Bahn kommt man schnell vom Stadtrand ins Zentrum.

....

....

....

e Auf dem Land kann man gut leben.

....

....

....

f Man baut dieses Hochhaus schnell.

....

....

....

C Prepositions with the dative case

> These prepositions are always followed by the dative case:
>
> *aus* (from, out of), *außer* (except for), *bei* (at), *gegenüber* (opposite), *mit* (with), *nach* (after, to), *seit* (since), *von* (from), *zu* (to)

5 Choose which preposition is right for each gap. The first gap has been filled for you.

> Ich komme **aus** der Türkei, aber ich wohne .... 3 Jahren in Berlin. Zuerst haben wir .... meiner Tante gewohnt, aber .... sechs Monaten haben wir eine Wohnung .... einer Kirche gemietet. Ich kann .... dem Bus .... meiner Schule fahren. Alle Bekannte .... meiner besten Freundin Aisha wohnen in der Nähe .... meiner Wohnung. Aisha wohnt in Ankara.

> Here are the dative endings for the definite and indefinite articles. As *ein* does not have a plural, the article *kein* (no, not any) is used for the plural.

	m	f	n	pl
Definite	dem	der	dem	den
Indefinite	einem	einer	einem	keinen

6 Select the correct article for each gap. The gender of the noun is given in brackets. Translate the phrases into English.

e.g. mit e......... Garage (f) → mit **einer** Garage (f): **with a garage**

a nach d......... Essen (n)

....

b aus d......... Küche (f)

....

c von e......... Freund (m)

....

d gegenüber d......... Häusern (pl)

e außer e......... Zimmer (n)

f seit e......... Woche (f)

g bei e......... Freundin (f)

h zu e......... Doppelhaus (n)

i in der Nähe von d......... Geschäften (pl)

> In both spoken and written German it is more usual to use these shortened forms:
>
> Masculine, neuter: zu dem → zum
>
>   bei dem → beim
>
>   von dem → vom
>
> Feminine: zu der → zur

7 Select which of the four shortened forms fit the sentences. Delete the others, as in the example.

> Ich wohne am Stadtrand. Heute habe ich einen Termin ~~zum~~/beim/~~vom~~/~~zur~~ Zahnarzt. Ich muss mit der Straßenbahn zum/beim/vom/zur Stadtrand zum/beim/vom/zur Stadtmitte fahren. Nachher werde ich zum/beim/vom/zur Büro von meinem Vater laufen. Er wird mich mit dem Auto zum/beim/vom/zur Schule fahren.

D Reflexive verbs

STUDENT BOOK 2.3 GRAMMAR SECTION D3

> A reflexive verb is used when the person doing the action does it to himself/herself:
>
> I wash myself.
> *Ich wasche mich.*
>
> I get (myself) dressed.
> *Ich ziehe mich an.*
>
> Reflexive verbs use reflexive pronouns, as follows:
>
> | ich | wasche **mich** | wir | waschen **uns** |
> |---|---|---|---|
> | du | wäschst **dich** | ihr | wascht **euch** |
> | er/sie | wäscht **sich** | Sie/sie | waschen **sich** |

8 These are reflexive verbs in the infinitive form. Match them to their English equivalents, as shown by the arrow.

a sich duschen   i   to have a shave
b sich treffen   ii   to enjoy oneself
c sich anziehen   iii to meet
d sich interessieren   iv   to shower
e sich freuen   v   to look forward (to)
f sich rasieren   vi   to hurry
g sich amüsieren   vii to be interested
h sich beeilen   viii to get dressed

9 Write the following reflexive verbs in the present tense giving the correct reflexive pronoun and the correct verb ending. Think about what each phrase means in English.

e.g. Du (*sich duschen*) → **Du duschst dich**

a Ich (*sich beeilen*)

b Wir (*sich interessieren*)

c Er (*sich rasieren*)

d Ihr (*sich treffen*)

e Meine Mutter (*sich duschen*)

f Ich (*sich anziehen*)

g Du (*sich amüsieren*)

h Wir (*sich beeilen*)

i Du (*sich interessieren*)

j Mein Vater und ich (*sich freuen*)

> Some verbs are used reflexively in the dative case. The dative is only different from the accusative in the *ich* and *du* forms. The dative forms are used when there is an object such as 'my hair' instead of the object 'myself'.
>
> *Ich putze **mir** die Zähne.* I clean my teeth.
>
> *Du wäschst **dir** die Haare.* You wash your hair.

Thema 2 Mein Zuhause

10 Translate these sentences about a group of friends on a school trip into German. They either need an accusative pronoun as in the last exercise, or a dative as explained above.

e.g. I shower at 8 o'clock. → **Ich dusche mich um acht Uhr.**

a We get dressed at 9 o'clock.

b I wash my hair every day.

c Hannes, are you interested?

d My friends are having fun.

e He cleans his teeth slowly.

f Where are we meeting today?

E Separable verbs

> The infinitive of separable verbs appears as one word (e.g. *aufstehen*) but the prefix (*auf-*) is separable. In the present tense you separate the prefix from the verb and put it at the end of the sentence. The main part of the verb must be the second idea in the sentence.
>
> *aufstehen* (to get up):
> *Ich stehe um 7 Uhr **auf**.*
>
> *fernsehen* (to watch television):
> *Wir sehen jeden Abend **fern**.*
>
> *anziehen* (to get dressed):
> *Sie zieht sich im Schlafzimmer **an**.*
>
> Some other useful separable verbs are:
>
> *abfahren* (to depart)
> *abwaschen* (to wash up)
> *ankommen* (to arrive)
> *anrufen* (to telephone)
> *aufräumen* (to tidy up)
> *einkaufen* (to shop)
> *saubermachen* (to clean)
> *vorbereiten* (to prepare)

11 Choose the correct prefix from the box to complete this text. The first gap has been filled for you.

> ab ab an an auf ein sauber vor

> Meine Eltern sind im Urlaub in Spanien, aber heute ist ihr letzter Tag. Sie fahren um 10 Uhr **ab** und kommen am Abend bei uns .... Jeden Tag rufen sie uns .... „Macht ihr alles ....?" fragt meine Mutter. Wir bereiten jetzt alles .... Ich kaufe im Supermarkt .... Mein Bruder wäscht .... und räumt im Wohnzimmer.............

12 All of these sentences contain separable verbs in the present tense. Rearrange them using correct word order and punctuation.

e.g. das/wir/auf/räumen/Wohnzimmer → **Wir räumen das Wohnzimmer auf.**

a in/fern/Schlafzimmer/ich/meinem/sehe

b auf/Geschäft/das/um/Uhr/macht/zehn

c kauft/im/ein/Sandra/gern/Stadtzentrum

d ein/Kinder/schlafen/müden/die/früh

e steigt/München/um/in/ihr

f dem/fern/sehen/wir/nach/Abendessen

Thema 3 Freizeit

A Word order: inversion

STUDENT BOOK 3.4 | GRAMMAR SECTION H1

> The position of the verb is very important in German sentences. The usual rule is that it must be the second idea in the sentence or clause, although not necessarily the second word. In these examples, the verb is shown in bold type:
>
> Ich **höre** gern Musik.
>
> Meine Schwester und ich **hören** gern Musik.
>
> Where the verb has two parts, for example when it is used in the perfect tense or if it is a separable verb in the present tense, the second part goes to the end:
>
> Ich **sehe** gern mit meiner Familie **fern**.

1 Make sure you can identify verbs. Underline the verb (both parts for separable verbs) in these sentences.

e.g. Ich <u>spiele</u> Trompete in einem Orchester.

Das Konzert <u>fängt</u> um sieben Uhr <u>an</u>.

a Meine Mutter fährt gleich in die Türkei.

b Sein Freund geht sehr oft ins Kino.

c Meine Freunde und ich kaufen samstags zusammen ein.

d Mein Bruder trifft seine Freundin vor dem Theater.

e Ich interessiere mich für Bücher.

f Wir gehen nur am Wochenende aus.

g Stefan und Luzie essen immer in einem Restaurant.

2 Rewrite these sentences with the word(s) in italics at the beginning, as in the example.

e.g Wir essen ein Eis *im Eiscafé*. → **Im Eiscafé essen wir ein Eis.**

a Das Konzert fängt *um sieben Uhr* an.

....

....

b Ich spiele *Trompete* in einem Orchester.

....

....

c Meine Mutter fährt *gleich* in die Türkei.

....

....

d Sein Freund geht *sehr oft* ins Kino.

....

....

e Meine Freunde und ich kaufen *samstags* zusammen ein.

....

....

f Mein Bruder trifft seine Freundin *vor dem Theater*.

....

....

B Time, manner, place

STUDENT BOOK 3.1 | GRAMMAR SECTION H2

> When you mention when (time), how (manner) and where (place) you do something, the order they take in a sentence is time, manner, place:
>
> Ich fahre nächstes Jahr mit dem Zug nach Deutschland.
>
> In English it sounds more natural if you say: 'I'm going to Germany next year by train', but in German it is important that you keep to this word order rule.

3 Rearrange these sentences using correct word order and starting with the subject each time. The punctuation will help you.

e.g. Hannover. morgen Ich mit fahre nach Bus dem → **Ich fahre morgen mit dem Bus nach Hannover.**

a 10 Zentrum. Wir mit kommen ins der Uhr S-Bahn um

....

....

b gehen Studenten Uni. zur zu Die Tag Fuß jeden

....

....

c zum Schwester Mutter geht Arzt. meiner Meine mit morgen

....

....

d komme glücklich dem Hause. nach nach Konzert sehr Ich

....

....

e mit Spanien. Meine Sommer nach fährt Auto Familie nächsten dem

....

....

f Straßenbahn immer Sie Fahren Hause? mit nach der

....

....

4 Rewrite sentences a–e (not f) from exercise 3, starting each sentence with the time element. You will have to change the order of the subject and the verb.

e.g. **Morgen fahre ich mit dem Bus nach Hannover.**

a ....

b ....

c ....

d ....

e ....

C Subordinating conjunctions

> Subordinating conjunctions introduce subordinate clauses. A subordinate clause gives more information about a main clause. Subordinating conjunctions send the verb to the end of the clause they introduce. Common subordinating conjunctions include:
>
> *da* (as, because), *dass* (that), *weil* (because), *wenn* (when, if), *damit* (so that), *als* (when: in past actions), *ob* (whether), *obwohl* (although), *bevor* (before), *nachdem* (after), *während* (while), *seitdem* (since), *so dass* (so that).
>
> You must use a comma before a subordinating conjunction.

5 Link the two sentences by making the second one a subordinate clause starting with the conjunction in brackets.

e.g. Ich finde es unfair. Ich bekomme kein Taschengeld. (*dass*) → **Ich finde es unfair, dass ich kein Taschengeld bekomme.**

a Ich habe keinen Nebenjob. Ich spiele samstags immer Fußball. (*weil*)

....

b Mein Bruder bekommt fünf Euro. Er wäscht das Auto. (*wenn*)

....

c Meine Eltern geben mir kein Geld. Sie sind ziemlich reich. (*obwohl*)

....

d Als Babysitterin bekomme ich das Geld. Das Ehepaar kommt nach Hause. (*nachdem*)

....

e Wir haben viel mehr Geld. Wir haben einen Nebenjob. (*seitdem*)

....

f Meine Schwester arbeitete in einem Supermarkt. Sie war jünger. (*als*)

....

g Ich weiß nicht. Ich bekomme diese Woche Taschengeld. (*ob*)

....

> If a subordinate clause has two verbs, e.g. a modal verb plus an infinitive or a verb used in the future or perfect tense, you have to think carefully about word order. It is the verb that would normally be the second idea in the sentence that goes right to the end. Look at what happens to the modal verb *muss* in the example:
>
> *Ich kaufe selten CDs. Ich **muss** Geld **sparen**.* →
>
> *Ich kaufe selten CDs, weil ich Geld **sparen muss.***
>
> If the verb in the subordinate clause is separable, such as the verb *aussehen* in the following example, the two parts are written as one word at the end of the clause:
>
> *Sie kauft neue Kleider. Sie **sieht** schön **aus**.* →
>
> *Sie kauft neue Kleider, damit sie schön **aussieht**.*

6 Link the two sentences by making the second one a subordinate clause starting with the conjunction in brackets. All of the subordinate clauses contain either two verbs or a separable verb.

e.g. Elke spart ihr Taschengeld. Sie kann Kleider kaufen. (*damit*) → **Elke spart ihr Taschengeld, damit sie Kleider kaufen kann.**

a Hannes verdient zehn Euro. Er räumt sein Zimmer auf. (*wenn*)

....

....

....

b Ich denke lange nach. Ich gebe Geld aus. (*bevor*)

....

....

....

c Er hört Musik auf einem MP3-Spieler. Er trägt Zeitungen aus. (*während*)

....

....

....

d Ich habe so viele Freunde. Meine Mutter muss mir Geld für ihre Geschenke geben. (*dass*)

....

....

....

7 When you have checked that your answers to exercise 6 are correct, rewrite a–c below with the subordinate clause first, as in the example. Remember the verb–comma–verb pattern.

e.g. Elke spart ihr Taschengeld damit sie Kleider kaufen kann. → **Damit sie Kleider kaufen kann, spart Elke ihr Taschengeld.**

a Wenn er ....

....

....

b ....

....

....

c ....

....

....

D Expressing preferences

> To say you like or don't like doing something, you can use *gern* or *nicht gern*. Although 'like' is a verb in English, *gern* isn't a verb but an adverb. It can be used alongside any verb and never changes:
>
> *Ich schwimme **gern**.*
>
> I like swimming.
>
> *Er spielt **nicht gern** Tennis.*
>
> He doesn't like playing tennis.
>
> The same principle applies to the word *lieber*, which you can use to say you prefer something, and *am liebsten* to say what you like best of all:
>
> *Ich spiele **gern** Fußball, aber ich spiele **lieber** Rugby und **am liebsten** spiele ich Handball.*
>
> I like playing football, but I prefer playing rugby and most of all I like playing handball.
>
> *Ich jogge **nicht gern**. Ich turne **noch weniger gern**. Ich mache Leichtathletik **überhaupt nicht gern**.*
>
> I don't like jogging. I like gymnastics even less. I really don't like doing athletics at all.
>
> To say you prefer to do one thing over another, use *lieber...als*:
>
> *Ich höre Popmusik **lieber als** Jazz.*
>
> I prefer pop music to jazz.

> There is no reason why a sentence cannot begin with a subordinate clause. If it does, the whole clause becomes the first idea in the sentence, and the verb in the main clause must come immediately after the comma in order to be the second idea.
>
> *Du **räumst** dein Zimmer **auf**. Du **bekommst** Taschengeld.* →
>
> *Wenn du dein Zimmer **aufräumst** [first idea], **bekommst** [second idea] du Taschengeld.*
>
> In sentences like this, there is always a verb–comma–verb pattern in the middle of the sentence:
>
> *...aufräumst, bekommst...*

8 Match up the pictures (a–f) with the statements (i–vi).

i Ich spiele Basketball lieber als Karate.

ii Ich spiele Tennis überhaupt nicht gern.

iii Ich spiele Basketball gern, aber ich spiele lieber Tischtennis.

iv Ich spiele Tischtennis weniger gern als Tennis.

v Ich mache Leichtathletik am liebsten.

vi Ich mache Karate am liebsten.

9 Write three sentences about your own preferences regarding sporting activities, using the sentences in exercise 8 as a model.

Thema 4 Die Schule

A Negation and negative forms

Kein can be placed before a noun to mean 'no', 'not a' or 'not any':

Ich habe ein Buch. I have a book.

*Ich habe **kein** Buch.* I have no book. (I don't have a book.)

Endings on *kein* follow the same pattern as the definite article, except that there is a plural form.

	m	f	n	pl
Nom	kein	keine	kein	keine
Acc	keinen	keine	kein	keine
Gen	keines	keiner	keines	keiner
Dat	keinem	keiner	keinem	keinen

The word *nicht* (not) is usually placed after the verb to make it negative, e.g. *Meine Schule ist **nicht** sehr groß*. Other useful negative words are *nie* (never), *nichts* (nothing) and *niemand* (no one). *Gar nichts* and *überhaupt nichts* both mean 'nothing at all'. Since *niemand* is a pronoun, it has different endings in the accusative (*niemanden*) and dative (*niemandem*).

1 Fill in the gaps with the correct word from the box. The first gap has been filled for you.

> nichts   keinen   kein   ~~nicht~~
> nie   keine   niemand

Meine Freundin hat viele Probleme in der Schule. Am Montag macht sie ihre Hausaufgaben **nicht**. Am Dienstag macht sie auch .... Hausaufgaben. Mittwochs, donnerstags und freitags macht sie auch gar .... Sie macht ihre Hausaufgaben .... ! Sie bringt .... Buch und .... Kuli mit in die Schule. Was kann man machen? Ich glaube, ... kann ihr helfen!

2 Choose the correct form of *kein* in these sentences. Think about the gender of the noun and the case, and whether it is singular or plural. Delete the forms that are wrong.

e.g. Mein deutscher Freund trägt ~~keinen~~/**keine**/~~kein~~ Schuluniform.

a Bei uns in der Schule gibt es keine/kein/keiner Kantine.

b Achtung! Kein/keine/keiner Schüler darf hier rauchen!

c Im Kindergarten hat man keiner/kein/keinen Stundenplan.

d Wir haben heute keinen/kein/keine Mittagessen gegessen.

e Keine/keinen/kein Lehrer tragen Jeans in dieser Schule.

B Adverbs and adverbial phrases of time

These words and phrases add interest to your writing and speaking, but also help you to work out time frames (past, present or future) when reading and listening. They include: *heute* (today), *gestern* (yesterday), *morgen* (tomorrow), *am Vormittag* (in the morning), *am Nachmittag* (in the afternoon), *am Abend* (in the evening), *jeden Tag* (every day), *letzte Woche* (last week), *nächsten Monat* (next month), *vor drei Jahren* (three years ago), *in drei Jahren* (in three years). When the phrases contain an adjective (e.g. **jeden** *Tag*), the adjective needs an accusative ending.

3 Translate these time phrases into German.

e.g. last year → **letztes Jahr**

a next year ....

b tomorrow evening ....

c yesterday afternoon ....

d next summer ....

e last winter ....

f next month ....

g tomorrow morning ....

h this (today) afternoon ....

i six weeks ago ....

C Perfect tense: weak verbs

The perfect tense is made up of two parts: the auxiliary verb (*haben* or *sein*) and the past participle. Word order: the auxiliary verb is the second idea and the past participle goes to the end of the sentence.

Past participles of weak (regular) verbs follow the same pattern. Remove the *-en* from the infinitive, replace it with a *-t* and add *ge-* to the start, e.g. *machen* → **ge**mach**t**.

*Sie **hat** ihre Hausaufgaben **gemacht**.*

She did her homework.

Most weak verbs use *haben* (in the present tense) as the auxiliary verb. Remember, the forms of *haben* are: *ich habe, du hast, er/sie/es/man hat, wir haben, ihr habt, Sie/sie haben.*

4 Complete the following sentences with the correct part of *haben* and the past participle of the weak verb given in brackets.

e.g. Ich .... Basketball .... (*spielen*)
→ Ich **habe** Basketball **gespielt**.

a Christoph .... viel Arbeit .... (*machen*)

b Ihr .... den Lehrer .... (*hören*)

c Wir .... letztes Jahr in Amerika .... (*wohnen*)

d Die Schüler .... in der Stunde nichts .... (*sagen*)

e Meine Freundin und ich .... neue Schulbücher .... (*kaufen*)

f Was .... Sie .... ? (*sagen*) Ich .... Sie leider nicht .... (*hören*)

g Wann .... du das .... ? (*machen*)

> If the stem of the verb ends in **-d** or **-t**, add **-et** at the end to form the past participle, e.g. *arbeiten* → *gearbeitet*. Verbs that already have a prefix such as **be-**, **emp-**, **ver-** in the infinitive (inseparable verbs) or which end in **-ieren** do not add **ge-** at the beginning to form the past participle, e.g. *telefonieren* → *telefoniert*, *besuchen* → *besucht*.

5 Rewrite these present tense sentences in the perfect tense, as in the example.

e.g. Die neue Lehrerin arbeitet nur nachmittags. →
Die neue Lehrerin hat nur nachmittags gearbeitet.

a Viele Schüler besuchen das Museum.

b Die letzte Stunde endet um halb vier.

c Telefonierst du mit der Lehrerin?

d Der Geschichtslehrer organisiert eine Klassenfahrt.

e Wir studieren an der Uni.

D Perfect tense: irregular (strong) and mixed verbs

> The past participles of irregular (strong) verbs also mostly have **ge-** at the beginning, unless the infinitive already has a prefix, but they end in **-en**, e.g. *geben* → *gegeben*. There may also be a vowel change, e.g. *trinken* → *getrunken*. As strong verbs are irregular by nature, you will have to consult the verb tables and learn the past participle for each verb individually.
>
> So-called 'mixed verbs' have a combination of weak and strong elements, e.g. *bringen* → *gebracht*. The vowel change makes this past participle irregular, but it still has a **-t** ending.

6 Use the verb tables at the back of this book to look up the past participles for these verbs.

e.g. essen → **gegessen**

a sprechen ....
b treffen ....
c sehen ....
d beginnen ....
e lesen ....
f schreiben ....
g denken ....
h wissen ....
i gehen ....
j fahren ....
k fliegen ....
l laufen ....

E Perfect tense: verbs taking *sein*

> If you look up the verbs *gehen*, *fahren*, *fliegen* and *laufen*, you will notice an asterisk (*) indicating that they take *sein* as an auxiliary verb. All verbs of movement from one place to another take *sein*, as do verbs that describe a change of state, e.g. *werden* (to become), *sterben* (to die).
>
> In addition to these two groups, the verb *bleiben* (to stay) also takes *sein*, e.g. *Ich bin geblieben* (I stayed). Remember the present tense forms of *sein* are: *ich bin, du bist, er/sie/es/man ist, wir sind, ihr seid, Sie/sie sind*.

7 Complete the sentences with the correct form of *sein* and the past participle of the verb given in brackets.

e.g. Er .... mit dem Rad zur Schule .... (*kommen*) → Er **ist** mit dem Rad zur Schule **gekommen**.

a Die sportlichen Schüler .... fünf Kilometer .... (*laufen*)

b Wir .... im Hallenbad .... (*schwimmen*)

c Ihr .... zu Fuß zur Schule .... (*gehen*)

d Du .... sehr müde .... (*werden*)

e Ich .... mit meiner Klasse nach Dänemark .... (*fahren*)

f Peter .... nach den Ferien nach Hause .... (*fliegen*)

g Meine Familie und ich .... in den Ferien zu Hause .... (*bleiben*)

h Ihr Großvater .... im Alter von 90 Jahren .... (*sterben*)

F Perfect tense: separable verbs

STUDENT BOOK 4.4 — GRAMMAR SECTION F3

> Some separable verbs are weak and others are strong. To form their past participle, you place the **ge-** after the separable prefix, e.g. *aufräumen* → *aufgeräumt*, *aufstehen* → *aufgestanden*.
>
> When you look up a separable verb in a verb table, you may only find the root verb. For example, to find the past participle of *anfangen* (to begin) you would look up *fangen* (past participle *gefangen*) and add the prefix **an-** to this (*angefangen*).
>
> Remember that not all prefixes are separable. If the infinitive begins with an inseparable prefix like **be-, ver-, ent-** the past participle does not require a **ge-**.

8 Here are some past participles. What is the infinitive of each verb? What do you notice about answers **d** and **h**?

e.g. angekommen → **ankommen**

a eingefahren ....

b angerufen ....

c umgezogen ....

d vergessen ....

e abgewaschen ....

f erfunden ....

g verstanden ....

h bekommen ....

i ausgegangen ....

9 Complete the passage below by writing the correct form of the verb given in brackets in the perfect tense. You will need to think about both the auxiliary verb and the past participle. The first verb has been done for you.

Der Schultag **hat** um 8.15 Uhr **angefangen** (*anfangen*).

Viele Schüler .... zu Fuß .... (*kommen*), aber ich .... mit dem Bus dorthin .... (*fahren*).

In der ersten Stunde .... wir Englisch .... (*lernen*) und nachher .... man Mathe .... (*machen*). In der Pause .... ich ein Käsebrot .... (*essen*) und Wasser .... (*trinken*). Mein Freund .... mir ein Geschenk .... (*mitbringen*). Das .... ich toll .... (*finden*). Leider .... ich mein Deutschbuch .... (*vergessen*) und ich .... nach der Deutschstunde im Klassenzimmer .... (*bleiben*), um mit dem Lehrer zu sprechen.

Thema 5 Berufe, Berufe...

A Masculine and feminine job titles

All German job titles have a masculine and a feminine form. Usually, you add *-in* to the masculine form, e.g. *der Lehrer → die Lehrerin*. Sometimes you also add an umlaut in the feminine form, e.g. *der Zahnarzt → die Zahnärztin*. If the masculine job title contains the word *-mann*, it changes to *-frau* for a woman, e.g. *der Geschäftsmann → die Geschäftsfrau*.

1 The words below are anagrams of job titles. Unjumble them and write the German next to its English meaning. Indicate whether it refers to a man (m) or a woman (f). Note: remember to write the noun with a capital letter.

stanwertchal	örrsif	tajnisloniru
nitiplorkie	rattizer	katrinahomeuce
tinpoil	höinck	
rintleshecmod	furreekvä	

e.g. doctor → **Ärztin** m/(f)

a hairdresser .... m / f
b sales assistant .... m / f
c solicitor .... m / f
d interpreter .... m / f
e vet .... m / f
f politician .... m / f
g journalist .... m / f
h pilot .... m / f
i car mechanic .... m / f
j cook .... m / f

You do not need an article when saying what someone does for a living:

Sie ist Polizistin. She is a policewoman.

2 Translate these sentences into German as in the example in the box.

a He is a bank clerk.
....

b I (f) am a bank clerk.
....

c Are you (formal, f) a hairdresser?
....

d My father is a teacher.
....

e You (informal, m) are a sales assistant.
....

f I am a businessman.
....

g Frau Henkel is a doctor.
....

h Is she a sales assistant?
....

B Infinitive constructions: *um...zu* and *ohne...zu*

To say 'in order to...' you use the construction *um...zu* and place the infinitive at the end of the clause. There is a comma before *um*:

Ich möchte Kindergärtnerin werden, um Kindern zu helfen.

I want to become a nursery assistant, in order to help children.

The phrase *ohne...zu* means 'without...', and also has a comma before it. The infinitive at the end of the clause often translates as something with '-ing' at the end in English:

Er hat meinen Brief gelesen, ohne mich zu fragen.

He read my letter without asking me.

In both these constructions, the *zu* comes just before the infinitive, unless it is a separable verb where it comes after the separable prefix, e.g. *um früh aufzustehen*.

3 Decide whether these sentences could be linked by *um...zu* or *ohne...zu*, and then rewrite them as one sentence.

e.g. Ich mache eine Ausbildung. Ich will Automechaniker werden. → **Ich mache eine Ausbildung, um Automechaniker zu werden.**

a Der Bäcker steht um 4.00 Uhr auf. Er backt Brot für die Bäckerei.
....
....
....

b Helga arbeitet in England. Sie will ihr Englisch verbessern.
....
....
....

c Wir können in der Nachtschicht arbeiten. Wir werden nicht müde.

   ....
   ....
   ....

d Frau Becker steht früh auf. Sie will ihre Arbeit früh anfangen.

   ....
   ....
   ....

e Mein Vater arbeitet den ganzen Tag im Büro. Er hat keine Pause.

   ....
   ....
   ....

C Infinitive constructions with and without *zu*

STUDENT BOOK **5.1** GRAMMAR SECTION **G2**

> The infinitive is used in a number of other constructions. In the following contexts there is **no need** to place *zu* before the verb:
> - after *ich gehe*, e.g. *ich gehe spazieren* (I go for a walk)
> - in combination with *lassen*, e.g. *sie lassen sich scheiden* (they are getting divorced)
> - after modal verbs e.g. *ich muss arbeiten* (I have to work)
> - with *werden* to form a future e.g. *er wird studieren* (he is going to study)
>
> You **do** need to place *zu* before the verb in other constructions expressing future intentions, such as:
> - *ich habe vor* (I intend)
> - *ich hoffe* (I hope)
> - *ich freue mich darauf* (I'm looking forward to)
>
> e.g. *Ich habe vor, Arzt zu werden.* I intend to become a doctor.

4 Do these pairs of sentences lead to the same outcome? Put a tick (✓) if they both mean the same thing and a cross (✗) if they mean something different.

   e.g. Nach dem Studium möchte ich als Ingenieur arbeiten.

   Ich habe vor, Ingenieur zu werden. ✓

a Ich lasse mein Auto in der Werkstatt reparieren.
   Der Mechaniker kann mein Auto nicht reparieren.

b Im Krankenhaus ist Rauchen verboten.
   Es ist nicht erlaubt, im Krankenhaus zu rauchen.

c Die Frisörin wäscht meine Haare.
   Beim Frisör lasse ich mir die Haare waschen.

d Wenn meine Schicht zu Ende ist, gehe ich schwimmen.
   Nach der Arbeit gehe ich ins Hallenbad.

e Wir freuen uns darauf, das Arbeitspraktikum zu beginnen.
   Wir denken, dass das Arbeitspraktikum keinen Spaß machen wird.

5 Go through the pairs of sentences a–e in exercise 4 and underline all the infinitives. There are five altogether. Copy them below and give a reason to explain why an infinitive is used each time.

   e.g. Nach dem Studium möchte ich als Ingenieur <u>arbeiten</u>.
   → **infinitive used after a modal verb** (*möchte*)

   Ich habe vor, Ingenieur zu <u>werden</u>. → **infinitive used after a verb of future intention** (*ich habe vor*)

i   ....
ii   ....
iii ....
iv   ....
v   ....

6 Do the sentences below require just an infinitive, or an infinitive with *zu*? Link the beginning of each sentence with the correct ending and write the English meaning in the space provided, as in the example.

   e.g. Ich wollte einen Teilzeitjob in einem Supermarkt… **iv**

   I wanted to get a part-time job in a supermarket.

a Es war aber nur möglich, einen Job als Verkäufer in einem Modegeschäft…

   ....
   ....

b Es ist meine Aufgabe, neue modische Kleidung…

   ....
   ....

c Ich muss sparen, also darf ich nicht zu viele Kleider selber…

   ....
   ....

d Ich habe vor, einen besseren Job als Manager…

....

....

e Am liebsten möchte ich im Ausland…

....

....

i …kaufen

ii …arbeiten

iii …zu finden

iv …~~bekommen~~

v …zu verkaufen

vi …zu suchen

D Cardinal numbers

GRAMMAR SECTION I1

> If you have to write numbers as words rather than digits in German, the most important thing to remember is that they are written as one word. This can make certain numbers, especially dates, appear incredibly long, but it is nevertheless correct.
>
> Here is a reminder of numbers in German:
>
> | | | |
> |---|---|---|
> | 0 *null* | | 40 *vierzig* |
> | 1 *eins* | 11 *elf* | 21 *einundzwanzig* | 50 *fünfzig* |
> | 2 *zwei* | 12 *zwölf* | 22 *zweiundzwanzig* | 60 *sechzig* |
> | 3 *drei* | 13 *dreizehn* | 23 *dreiundzwanzig* | 70 *siebzig* |
> | 4 *vier* | 14 *vierzehn* | 24 *vierundzwanzig* | 80 *achtzig* |
> | 5 *fünf* | 15 *fünfzehn* | 25 *fünfundzwanzig* | 90 *neunzig* |
> | 6 *sechs* | 16 *sechzehn* | 26 *sechsundzwanzig* | 100 *hundert* |
> | 7 *sieben* | 17 *siebzehn* | 27 *siebenundzwanzig* | 200 *zweihundert* |
> | 8 *acht* | 18 *achtzehn* | 28 *achtundzwanzig* | 1.000 *tausend* |
> | 9 *neun* | 19 *neunzehn* | 29 *neunundzwanzig* | 2.000 *zweitausend* |
> | 10 *zehn* | 20 *zwanzig* | 30 *dreißig* | 1.000.000 *eine Million* |
>
> To avoid confusion between *zwei* and *drei*, *zwo* is often used for the number 2 on the telephone and in public announcements.
>
> Here are some examples of dates:
>
> 1989: *neunzehnhundertneunundachtzig*
>
> 1992: *neunzehnhundertzweiundneunzig*
>
> 2004: *zweitausendvier*
>
> 2016: *zweitausendsechzehn*

7 Say these numbers out loud and then write them as digits.

e.g. dreihundertneunzehn → **319**

a viertausendachtundsiebzig ....

b neunhundertsiebenundzwanzig ....

c sechshundertzwölf ....

d zwohunderteinundachtzig ....

e fünftausenddreihundertzehn ....

f tausendeinhundertzweiundvierzig ....

g sechstausendneunhundertdreiundneunzig ....

8 Write out these years as words.

e.g. 1972 → **neunzehnhundertzweiundsiebzig**

a 1945 ....

....

b 2010 ....

....

c 1964 ....

....

d 1879 ....

....

e 2021 ....

....

f 1735 ....

....

g 2017 ....

....

Thema 6 ...und in Zukunft?

A Future tense

STUDENT BOOK 6.1 | GRAMMAR SECTION F6

In German, as in English, the present tense is often used to express future ideas if a future time phrase is included:

  *Ich **beginne nächste Woche** eine neue Stelle.*

  I'm going to start a new job next week.

Remember there are other expressions that express future intentions, such as *ich habe vor* (I intend), *ich hoffe* (I hope):

  *Ich **habe vor**, im Ausland zu studieren.*

  I intend to study abroad. (See also Thema 5, section C)

To form the future tense, use the correct form of the present tense of *werden* plus the infinitive of the relevant verb. This infinitive goes at the end of the sentence:

  *Ich **werde** Deutsch **studieren**.*

  I'm going to study German.

werden	
ich werde	wir werden
du wirst	ihr werdet
er/sie/es/man wird	Sie/sie werden

1 Read the sentences below and answer questions i–iii, then translate each one into English. The first has been done for you.

i Which sentences use the future tense with *werden*? (× 2) a ....

ii Which ones use the present tense, but show future intention? (× 4) ....

iii Which ones use the present tense of *werden* in the sense of 'to become'? (× 2) ....

a Stefan wird sich für eine Stelle als Mechaniker bewerben.
→ **Stefan is going to apply for a job as a mechanic.**

b Nächste Woche fängt die Uni wieder an.
....
....

c Nach einem langen Arbeitstag werde ich immer sehr müde.
....
....

d Wir haben vor, in den USA Geschichte zu studieren.
....
....

e Was wirst du nach dem Abitur machen?
....
....

f Jedes Jahr wird es schwieriger, einen Studienplatz zu bekommen.
....
....

g Ich habe morgen ein Interview bei dieser Firma.
....
....

h Die Schüler haben die Absicht, ein Praktikum zu machen.
....
....

2 Answer the questions using the future tense with *werden*, as in the example.

e.g. Arbeitet Ihre Schwester jetzt schon als Krankenschwester? (nach ihren Prüfungen) → **Nein, sie wird nach ihren Prüfungen als Krankenschwester arbeiten**.

a Fängst du dein Studium im August an? (im September)
....
....

b Macht Jochen das Abitur dieses Jahr? (nächstes Jahr)
....
....

c Studierst du jetzt schon Englisch? (nach den Ferien)
....
....

d Macht ihr beide eine Berufsausbildung? (in Zukunft)
....
....

e Dauert diese Ausbildung zwei Jahre? (noch ein Jahr)
....
....

B Adverbs and adverbial phrases for degrees of certainty

> Adverbs, and adverbial phrases, can express how likely something is to happen. Examples of these suggesting 'perhaps' or 'possibly' are: *vielleicht*, *eventuell* and *möglicherweise*. All of them suggest that something might happen, but isn't definite. Note that *eventuell* is a false friend for English speakers and means 'perhaps', **not** 'eventually'. 'Definitely' could be *bestimmt* or *auf jeden Fall*, while 'definitely not' could be *auf keinen Fall* or *bestimmt nicht*.
>
> Remember, if you start the sentence with an adverb or adverbial phrase, you need to invert the verb.

3 Rearrange these words to form sentences starting with the adverb or adverbial phrase, then translate them into English.

e.g. ich/Ausland/studieren/werde/möglicherweise/im →
Möglicherweise werde ich im Ausland studieren. →
I will possibly study abroad.

a macht/eventuell/er/Lehre/als/eine/Frisör

....

....

....

b möchte/werden/Zahnarzt/Ferdinand/auf keinen Fall

....

....

....

c Berufsausbildung/an/fange/ich/vielleicht/eine/im Herbst

....

....

....

d Zukunft/Bank/in/arbeiten/du/einer/wahrscheinlich/in/wirst

....

....

....

e suchen/auf jeden Fall/Teilzeitjob/Kellnerin/als/sie/wird/einen

....

....

....

4 On a separate piece of paper, write three sentences in German about your own future using adverbs or adverbial phrases of certainty. Say what you will possibly, definitely and definitely not do in the next 5 years. Use the sentences in exercise 3 as a model if you need some ideas.

C Modes of address

> There are three pronouns for 'you' in German: *du*, *ihr* and *Sie*.
>
> *Du* is used for a child or for someone you know well, such as a family member or friend. You would also address a pet as *du*.
>
> The pronoun *ihr* is the plural of *du*, so is used when you address more than one child, or more than one person you know well.
>
> *Sie* is the formal form of 'you' and can be either singular or plural. It is used by children when addressing one or more adults outside of their family and friends, and amongst adults in a more formal setting such as in a business meeting. It is important to write the formal *Sie* pronoun with a capital letter.

5 Circle the pronoun you would use if you were addressing:

e.g. your German penfriend — (du)/ihr/Sie

a both of your penfriend's parents when you arrive in Germany — du/ihr/Sie

b your aunt — du/ihr/Sie

c both your grandparents — du/ihr/Sie

d your penfriend's guinea pig — du/ihr/Sie

e your employer — du/ihr/Sie

f a class of children in school — du/ihr/Sie

g your teacher in school — du/ihr/Sie

h a group of your teachers — du/ihr/Sie

i a group of your friends — du/ihr/Sie

j your cat — du/ihr/Sie

k both of your cats together — du/ihr/Sie

l a shop assistant — du/ihr/Sie

6 Look at the ending of the verb to work out whether to add *du*, *ihr* or *Sie* in each sentence.

e.g. Was machst .... nach dem Abitur? → Was machst **du** nach dem Abitur?

a Ich glaube, ... haben eine Vollzeitstelle bei der Polizei.

b Hast .... schon Arbeitserfahrung?

c Wollt .... lieber in der Küche oder im Restaurant arbeiten?

d Wissen .... , wie viel man hier verdient?

e Es wäre eine gute Idee, wenn .... im Team arbeitet.

f Sind .... zuverlässig und fleißig?

D Forming questions

> Questions can be formed by inversion of the verb. This means you place the verb first and the subject second:
>
> *Sie **rufen** mich um 10 Uhr **an**.*
>
> You are ringing me at 10 o'clock.
>
> ***Rufen** Sie mich um 10 Uhr **an**?*
>
> Will you ring me at 10 o'clock?
>
> Questions can also begin with a question word, in which case the verb remains as the second idea:
>
> ***Wann** rufen Sie mich an?*
>
> When are you ringing me?
>
> Useful interrogative or question words are: *wann?* (when?), *wer?* (who?), *wo?* (where?), *was?* (what?), *wie?* (how?), *warum?* (why?), *wie viele?* (how many?), *um wie viel Uhr?* (at what time?)

7 Match up questions and answers.

a	Wer ist das?	**i**	Ungefähr dreißig.
b	Was macht er?	**ii**	Der Manager.
c	Um wie viel Uhr beginnt die Schicht?	**iii**	Er muss die Nachtschicht arbeiten.
d	Wo arbeitet er normalerweise?	**iv**	Zwei Jahre schon.
e	Wie viele Arbeiter gibt es dort?	**v**	In einer Fabrik.
f	Wie findet er die Arbeit?	**vi**	Um 21 Uhr.
g	Seit wann arbeitet er hier?	**vii**	Er muss Probleme lösen.
h	Warum ist er so müde?	**viii**	Es gefällt ihm gut.

8 Translate these questions into German as if for a job interview.

e.g. Would you like to work here? → **Möchten Sie hier arbeiten?**

a Why would you like to work here?

b Where have you already worked?

c At what time did you start?

d How did you find this job?

e Do you have experience?

f What would you like to do in the future?

g When can you begin?

h How much do you want to earn?

E Interrogative adjectives

> The question word *welcher* means 'which' and declines like *der/die/das*.
>
> | | m | f | n | pl |
> |---|---|---|---|---|
> | **Nom** | welcher | welche | welches | welche |
> | **Acc** | welchen | welche | welches | welche |

9 Insert the correct form of *welcher* into these sentences. Remember it needs to agree in gender, number and case.

e.g. .... Studentin hat diese Teilzeitstelle bekommen? → **Welche** Studentin hat diese Teilzeitstelle bekommen?

a .... Frau hat heute angerufen?

b .... Tag ist besser für diesen Termin?

c Ich weiß nicht, ... Leute hier arbeiten.

d .... Buch liegt auf dem Tisch?

e Ich bin nicht sicher, ... Sprache er spricht.

f .... Brief haben Sie zur Post gebracht?

F Saying and writing German dates

 GRAMMAR SECTION I2

The question words *wie viel* are turned into a noun with adjective endings when used to ask the question: 'What is the date today?' There are two ways of doing this in German:

Der Wievielte ist heute? (nominative)

Den Wievielten haben wir heute? (accusative)

Your answer will depend on which question was used:

Der Wievielte ist heute? Heute ist **der** zehn**te** Mai.

Den Wievielten haben wir heute?
Heute haben wir **den** zehn**ten** Mai.

To make ordinal numbers (10th, 6th etc.) up to **19th** you usually add *-te* to the cardinal number, e.g. *zehnte*, *sechste*.

There are a few exceptions, such as: *erste* (first), *dritte* (third), *siebte* (seventh), *achte* (eighth).

From **20th** upwards, add *-ste* to the cardinal number: *zwanzigste* (20th), *einunddreißigste* (31st), *hundertste* (100th).

---

10 Complete these dates as in the example, writing out the numbers as words.

e.g. Heute ist ....
(9 February) → Heute ist **der neunte Februar**.

a Heute haben wir .... (20 June)

b Heute haben wir .... (5 December)

c Heute ist .... (30 October)

d Heute haben wir .... (2 January)

e Heute ist .... (1 May)

f Heute ist .... (3 March)

When you write the date using a digit, you replace the ending *-te(n)* or *-ste(n)* with a dot:

den vierzehnten August → *den 14. August*

If you were writing a letter, you would usually write your location, a comma, then the abbreviated version of the date in the accusative case at the top of the page: *Hamburg, den 25. September 2015.*

---

11 Rewrite the dates from exercise 10 using the abbreviated form as if you were writing a letter. Find the name of a different German town to include in each one and make up the year, as in the example.

e.g. **München, den 9. Februar 2015**

a ....

b ....

c ....

d ....

e ....

f ....

To give information about a date on which something is happening, e.g. 'on 15 November', use *am* plus a dative ending on the number:

Mein Geburtstag ist **am** *elf***ten** *Dezember.*

My birthday is on 11 December.

Am *vier***ten** *Juli um elf Uhr habe ich schon einen Termin.*

I already have an appointment on 4 July at 11 o'clock.

---

12 Write these dates in full using *am*.

e.g. on 19 April → **am neunzehnten April**

a on 8 June ....

b on 31 December ....

c on 26 January ....

d on 1 September ....

e on 3 August ....

Thema 7 Unterwegs

A Imperative

STUDENT BOOK 7.2 | **GRAMMAR SECTION F2**

The imperative is used when you want to give instructions or orders. The imperative of the polite form *Sie* is the same as the present tense, but you place the *Sie* after the verb:

> **Gehen Sie** *geradeaus*. Go straight on.
>
> **Nehmen Sie** *die erste Straße links*. Take the first road on the left.

To make the imperative of the *du* form, take off the *-(e)st* of the present tense. You do not include the word *du*:

> **Geh** *geradeaus*.
>
> **Nimm** *die erste Straße links*.

Verbs that usually have an umlaut in the *du* form do not keep it in the imperative:

> **fahr!** drive!   **schlaf!** sleep!

In the *ihr* form, the imperative is the *ihr* form of the verb without the pronoun:

> **Geht** *geradeaus*.
>
> **Nehmt** *die erste Straße links*.

An important exception is *sein*:

> **Seien Sie** ruhig! (*Sie* form), **Seid** ruhig! (*ihr* form), **Sei** ruhig! (*du* form) = Be quiet!

Separable verbs keep their prefix separate:

> einfahren → **Fahren Sie** in den Parkplatz **ein**.

1 Fill in the gaps in these directions with the imperative form of the verb given in brackets.

e.g. Use the *Sie* form: .... (*kommen*) schnell! → **Kommen Sie** schnell!

a Use the *Sie* form:

> .... (*gehen*) geradeaus bis zur Haltestelle und dann .... (*fahren*) mit dem Bus weiter. Am Bahnhof .... (*aussteigen*).

b Use the *du* form:

> .... (*gehen*) um die Ecke und .... (*suchen*) eine kleine Kirche. Vor der Kirche .... in die Straßenbahn Linie 7 .... (*einsteigen*). .... (*fahren*) bis zur Stadtmitte.

c Use the *ihr* form:

> .... (*fahren*) mit dem Zug nach Lübeck. Dann .... (*gehen*) zu Fuß weiter. .... (*kommen*) aus dem Hauptbahnhof und .... (*nehmen*) die dritte Straße rechts.

The infinitive can be used to give general commands such as one sometimes sees on doors or in buildings:

> Bitte **ziehen**. Please pull.
>
> Nicht **rauchen**. No smoking.

It is also commonly used in instructions such as recipes:

> Kartoffeln **schälen** und in Würfel **schneiden**.
> Peel and dice the potatoes.

This form is also found on self-service machines:

> Geld **einwerfen**. Insert the money.

When using public transport in Germany you often have to validate your ticket before travelling by stamping it in a machine which says '*Fahrscheine* **entwerten**'.

2 The following commands are very useful. Some are used colloquially in everyday speech and others might be heard on public transport.

i Match up the German and English meanings.

ii Identify whether an imperative form or the infinitive is used for each one, as in the first example.

				Imp/Inf
a	Schlaf gut!	i	Stand back please.	**Imp**
b	Hör auf!	ii	Listen.	
c	Rufen Sie doch mal an!	iii	Help me.	
d	Bitte einsteigen!	iv	Sleep well.	
e	Zurücktreten bitte!	v	Don't be stupid.	
f	Sei nicht dumm!	vi	Turn off mobile phones.	
g	Hört zu!	vii	Stop it.	
h	Fahrausweis bitte vorzeigen!	viii	Make a phone call.	
i	Handys ausschalten!	ix	Please get on (the train/bus).	
j	Hilf mir!	x	Please show your ticket.	

B Zum/zur

The preposition *zu* is always followed by the dative case.

	m	f	n	pl
Dat	dem	der	dem	den

When used with masculine and neuter nouns, the preposition *zu* and article *dem* are usually shortened to *zum*. Similarly in the feminine form, *zu der* is usually shortened to *zur*. This contraction is particularly useful when asking for directions to a place. In the plural, *zu den* is never shortened.

Other prepositions taking the dative case are covered in more detail in *Thema* 8.

3 Insert *zum*, *zur* or *zu den* in these questions or instructions. You may need to check the gender of the noun.

e.g. Wie komme ich .... Bahnhof? → Wie komme ich **zum** Bahnhof?

a Wie komme ich .... Hallenbad?

b Gehen Sie bis .... Ampel.

c Wie komme ich .... Zoo?

d Ist es weit von hier .... Geschäften?

e Wie komme ich .... Haltestelle?

f Geh diese Straße entlang bis .... Taxis, die vor dem Bahnhof warten.

g Fahrt .... Stadtmitte und dann steigt aus.

h Wie fahre ich .... nächsten Parkhaus?

i Ist es weit bis .... U-Bahn-Station?

C Modal verbs *können*, *wollen*, *sollen*

There are six so-called 'modal verbs' in German. *Können*, *wollen* and *sollen* are three of them, and you use these verbs to say what you can do (*können*), want to do (*wollen*) or should do (*sollen*). They are always combined with another verb in the infinitive form. This is how you conjugate the verbs in the present tense:

	können	wollen	sollen
ich	kann	will	soll
du	kannst	willst	sollst
er/sie/es/man	kann	will	soll
wir	können	wollen	sollen
ihr	könnt	wollt	sollt
Sie/sie	können	wollen	sollen

In a main clause, the modal verb takes up the usual position of the verb as the second idea, and the infinitive of the second verb goes to the end:

*Ich **will** nach Italien **fahren**.*

I want to go to Italy.

In a subordinate clause, the modal verb goes to the end:

*Ich buche einen Flug, weil ich nach Italien **fahren will**.*

I am booking a flight because I want to go to Italy.

4 Complete this dialogue in the tourist information centre using the correct form of the modal verb in brackets. The first verb has been done for you.

A Guten Tag, **kann** (*können*) ich Ihnen helfen?

B Ja. Ich .... (*wollen*) eine Stadtrundfahrt mit meinem Sohn, Theo, machen.

A Kein Problem. Was .... (*wollen*) Sie sehen?

B Ich weiß nicht. Was .... (*sollen*) man hier sehen?

A Also, Sie .... (*können*) eine längere Rundfahrt machen, um den Dom, das Schloss und die historischen Gärten zu besuchen. Da .... (*können*) man aussteigen, wann und wo man .... (*wollen*). Mit Kindern .... (*sollen*) man unbedingt ins Puppenmuseum gehen.

B Was meinst du, Theo, ... (*wollen*) wir ins Museum gehen?

C .... (*können*) ich mit den Puppen spielen?

A Nein, leider nicht. Aber du .... (*können*) Puppen im Geschäft kaufen, wenn du .... (*wollen*).

B Danke für diese Information. .... (*sollen*) ich die Karten für die Rundfahrt hier kaufen?

A Wenn Sie .... (*wollen*), ... (*können*) Sie die Karten bei mir kaufen. Oder man .... (*können*) sie auch im Bus bekommen.

D The genitive case (possession)

The genitive case is used mainly to show possession, e.g. 'the woman's house' would need to be rephrased as 'the house of the woman' and then translated using the genitive feminine article: *das Haus **der** Frau*.

If you wanted to say 'the man's house' ('the house of the man'), you would use the genitive masculine article, but in the neuter and masculine you also need to add -*s* or -*es* to the noun, e.g. *das Haus **des** Mann**es***.

If there is an apostrophe showing possession in the English, you probably need to use the genitive in German.

	m	f	n	pl
Genitive definite article	des	der	des	der
Genitive indefinite article	eines	einer	eines	—
	keines	keiner	keines	keiner

The genitive is also used after certain prepositions, including *außerhalb* (outside [of]), *innerhalb* (within/inside), *statt* (instead of), *trotz* (in spite of), *während* (during), *wegen* (because of):

> *trotz des Wetters*
> despite the weather

5 *Wollen Sie Stadtführer werden?* If you wanted a job as a town guide, you would have to know facts such as those listed below. Translate them into German using the genitive. The nouns and genders are given in brackets.

e.g. the history of the castle (*die Geschichte; das Schloss*) → **die Geschichte des Schlosses**

a the height of the tower (*die Höhe; der Turm*)

....

....

b the length of the river (*die Länge; der Fluss*)

....

....

c the name of the town (*der Name; die Stadt*)

....

....

d the number of inhabitants (*die Anzahl; die Einwohner*)

....

....

e the price of an entrance ticket (*der Preis; die Eintrittskarte*)

....

....

f the age of the church (*das Alter; die Kirche*)

....

....

g the age of the cathedral (*das Alter; der Dom*)

....

....

h the location of the toilets (*die Lage; die Toiletten*)

....

....

6 Fill in the gaps in this text about local transport with the correct form of the genitive article. The first one has been done for you.

Am kommenden Wochenende kann es wegen **eines** Stadtfestes zu Problemen im Stadtverkehr kommen. Innerhalb d....... Innenstadt gibt es keine Parkmöglichkeiten für Autos. Während d....... ganzen Wochenendes bleibt die Innenstadt verkehrsfrei. Stadtfestbesucher, die außerhalb d....... Stadt wohnen, können statt d....... Autos einen kostenlosen Bus benutzen. Trotz d....... hohen Anzahl von Reisenden werden Sie genug Plätze im Bus finden.

Thema 8 Ferien

A Prepositions that always take the accusative

These prepositions always take the accusative case:

für (for)	für **meine** Mutter (for my mother)
um ((a)round)	um **die** Ecke (round the corner)
durch (through)	durch **die** Tür (through the door)
gegen (against)	gegen **unsere** Mannschaft (against our team)
entlang (along — stands after the noun)	**den** Gang entlang (along the corridor)
bis (until, by)	bis komm**enden** Montag (by next Monday)
ohne (without)	ohne **einen** Grund (without a reason)
wider (against)	wider **das** Gesetz (against the law)

The first letter of each preposition above combines to make up the acronym FUDGEBOW. This might help you to remember them.

Note: *wider* is not very common today. You might still come across it in a phrase such as *wider meinen Willen* (against my will); use *gegen* for 'against'.

Here is a reminder of accusative endings for the definite and indefinite articles:

	m	f	n	pl
Definite (acc)	den	die	das	die
Indefinite (acc)	einen	eine	ein	keine

1 Translate these phrases into German using the nouns in the box.

Badezimmer (n)	Mann (m)	Straße (f)
Dusche (f)	Parkplatz (m)	Stunde (f)
Kinder (pl)	Rat (m)	Wand (f)

e.g. against a wall → **gegen eine Wand**

a for an hour ....
b without my husband ....
c along the street ....
d through the car park ....
e against my advice ....
f without a shower ....
g without a bathroom ....
h through the wall ....
i for the children ....

2 Add the correct endings to the articles and possessive adjectives in this dialogue in a tourist information office. The first one has been done for you.

Kunde	Ich suche ein Doppelzimmer für mich und mein**en** Mann, und ein Einzelzimmer für mein........ Tochter.
Angestellter	Ja, das Hotel zum Schwan hat Zimmer frei. Ein Doppelzimmer für Sie und Ihr........ Mann und ein Einzelzimmer für Ihr........ Tochter. Sind Sie mit dem Auto hier?
Kunde	Nein, wir sind zu Fuß unterwegs.
Angestellter	Gut. Ohne d........ Auto ist es viel leichter zu finden. Gehen Sie durch d........ Fußgängerzone bis d........ Eingang zum Einkaufszentrum. Dort gehen Sie rechts um d........ Gebäude herum und dann d........ Weg entlang. Auf der linken Seite sehen Sie das Hotel.

B Prepositions that always take the dative

These prepositions are always followed by the dative case: *aus* (from, out of), *außer* (except for), *bei* (at [someone's house]), *gegenüber* (opposite), *mit* (with), *nach* (after, to), *seit* (since), *von* (from), *zu* (to):

mit **dem** Taxi   nach **dem** Abendessen

Note: in the plural, nouns also take an -n ending when used after a dative preposition:

außer **den** Kinder**n**

Here is a reminder of dative endings for the definite and indefinite articles:

	m	f	n	pl
Definite (acc)	dem	der	dem	den
Indefinite (acc)	einem	einer	einem	keinen

3 Using the vocabulary given in the box for exercise 1 above, translate these phrases into German.

e.g. opposite the bathroom → **gegenüber dem Badezimmer**

a from the street ....
b with a shower ....
c after an hour ....
d to the car park ....
e opposite the wall ....
f except for the man ....
g out of the car park ....
h to the street ....
i for (since) an hour ....
j at the house of the children ....

> When *zu*, *bei* and *von* are followed by the definite article, the shortened forms are used:
>
> zu dem → zum   zu der → zur
> bei dem → beim   von dem → vom

4 Add the correct endings to the articles and possessive adjectives in this description of a journey. In two places you will need to use the shortened form after *zu*. The first one has been done for you.

> Um acht Uhr früh gehe ich aus mein**em** Haus. Ich werde das Wochenende bei mein........ Großeltern in Hameln verbringen. Mit d........ Bus fahre ich zu........ Stadtmitte und dann gehe ich zu Fuß weiter zu........ Bahnhof. Von mein........ Stadt nach Hameln sind es nur 20 Minuten mit d........ Bahn. Nach d........ kurzen Reise steige ich aus. Ich habe meine Großeltern seit ein........ Monat nicht gesehen und ich bin sehr froh, sie zu sehen. Dort warten sie, gegenüber d........ Café.

C Prepositions taking either accusative or dative

STUDENT BOOK 8.2   GRAMMAR SECTION E3

> Some prepositions can be followed by either the accusative or the dative: *an* (at, on [vertical things, e.g. *an der Wand*]), *auf* (on [horizontal things, e.g. *auf dem Tisch*]), *hinter* (behind), *in* (in, into), *neben* (next to), *über* (over, above, across), *unter* (under, among), *vor* (in front of), *zwischen* (between).
>
> Decide which case is needed according to how the preposition is used in each context.

> For example, the preposition *in* is followed by the accusative when it means 'into' and the dative when it means 'in', i.e. if describing where something is situated. The accusative is used to show movement towards a place, the dative is used to show rest or position at a place.
>
> Shortened forms: in das → ins   in dem → im
>
> an das → ans   an dem → am
>
> auf das → aufs

5 Read these sentences and decide whether the preposition in each one is followed by the accusative or the dative. Delete the case that doesn't apply. Then translate the sentences into English.

e.g. Belgien liegt zwischen den Niederlanden und Frankreich.   ~~Acc~~/Dat

→ **Belgium is situated between the Netherlands and France.**

a Gehen Sie über die Kreuzung.   Acc/Dat
....
....

b Wir machen dieses Jahr Urlaub auf dem Land.   Acc/Dat
....
....

c Meine Tante hat eine Ferienwohnung am Meer.   Acc/Dat
....
....

d Das Hotel liegt neben dem Zoo.   Acc/Dat
....
....

e Setzen Sie meine Tasche bitte vor die Zimmertür.   Acc/Dat
....
....

f Wir fahren zum Skifahren in die Schweiz.   Acc/Dat
....
....

g Am ersten August fahren wir los!   Acc/Dat
....
....

h In den Bergen ist es sehr ruhig.   Acc/Dat
....
....

i Am liebsten fahre ich an die Ostsee.   Acc/Dat
....
....

6 This paragraph about holiday plans includes a variety of prepositions. Decide which case is required for each and delete the word that is in the wrong case, as in the first example.

> Dieses Jahr machen wir in ~~die~~/den Sommerferien etwas Spannendes. Ich fliege mit meine/meiner Familie in die/den Vereinigten Staaten. Aber wir fahren ohne meinen/meinem Bruder, weil er arbeiten muss. Er hat schon vor ein/einem Jahr eine Reise quer durch das/dem Land gemacht. Ins/Im Flugzeug möchte ich neben das/dem Fenster sitzen, um eine schöne Aussicht auf die/der Stadt zu haben, wenn wir in New York landen.

D Imperfect tense (of *sein, haben, es gibt*)

STUDENT BOOK 8.3 — GRAMMAR SECTION F4

The imperfect tense is used to describe past events or situations. Even when a speaker is using the perfect tense, the verbs *haben* and *sein*, as well as the impersonal construction *es gibt*, are often found in the imperfect.

haben	
ich hatte	wir hatten
du hattest	ihr hattet
er/sie/es/man hatte	Sie/sie hatten

sein	
ich war	wir waren
du warst	ihr wart
er/sie/es/man war	Sie/sie waren

es gibt (there is, there are) → *es gab* (there was, there were)

7 Rewrite sentences from a holiday postcard in the imperfect tense.

e.g. Heute ist ein schöner Tag! → **Heute war ein schöner Tag!**

a Ich bin mit meiner Familie in Italien.

b Wir sind mit unserem Wohnwagen hier.

c Der Campingplatz ist sehr groß.

d Er hat zwei Schwimmbäder.

e Es gibt auch einen Tennisplatz.

f Wir haben viel zu tun.

g Meine Geschwister sind am Abend müde.

h Seid ihr auch im Urlaub?

i Habt ihr auch viel Spaß dort?

> *Es gibt*, and the imperfect *es gab*, need to be followed by the accusative:
>
> *Es gab **einen** Fernseher im Zimmer.*

8 These sentences are all in the imperfect and refer to a bad experience on holiday. Match up the sentence beginnings (a–h) and endings (i–viii) to show what went wrong. It may help to check genders of nouns in a dictionary.

a	Ich war sehr…	**i**	…Toilettenpapier.
b	Es war kein…	**ii**	…schlechte Aussicht.
c	Mein Zimmer hatte…	**iii**	…unzufrieden.
d	Es gab einen…	**iv**	…kaputte Dusche.
e	Im Badezimmer gab es kein…	**v**	…Handtücher.
f	Vom Fenster gab es eine…	**vi**	…schöner Urlaub.
g	Wir hatten dreckige…	**vii**	…keine Lampe.
h	Es gab eine…	**viii**	…kaputten Fernseher.

Thema 9 Gesundheit

A Comparative adjectives and adverbs

STUDENT BOOK 9.2 **GRAMMAR SECTION** B8

> To compare two things you use the comparative form of the adjective. This is formed by adding *-er* to the adjective, e.g. *klein → kleiner* (small → smaller). A one-syllable adjective with a vowel (a, o or u) will usually take an umlaut in the comparative form, e.g. *groß → größer* (big → bigger), *alt → älter* (old → older). This occasionally happens with longer adjectives too, e.g. *gesund → gesünder* (healthy → healthier).
>
> There are some exceptions, such as *viel → mehr* (lots → more), *gut → besser* (good → better), *hoch → höher* (high → higher).
>
> The comparative can also be used as an adverb:
>
> *Er singt gut. → Sie singt besser.*

1 Two friends, Toni and Peter, are showing off about what they do to lead a healthy lifestyle. Peter is trying to outdo Toni by doing everything slightly better, in his opinion. Take the part of Peter and fill in his part in the conversation, using the example as a guide.

Toni	Ich esse wenig Fett.
Peter	**Ich esse weniger Fett.** *(example)*
Toni	Ich stehe früh auf, um zu trainieren.
Peter	....
Toni	Ich trinke selten Kaffee.
Peter	....
Toni	Ich treibe oft Sport.
Peter	....
Toni	Ich bleibe lang im Fitnesszentrum.
Peter	....
Toni	Ich komme spät vom Fitnesszentrum zurück.
Peter	....
Toni	Ich esse viel Obst.
Peter	....
Toni	Ich lebe gesund.
Peter	....
Toni	Mein Lebensstil ist gut.
Peter	....

> Comparative adjectives can also go in front of the noun, in which case they take the usual adjective endings:
>
> *Peter versucht, ein **gesünderes** Leben zu führen.*
> Peter is trying to live a healthier life.

2 Translate these sentences into English.

e.g. Wir essen jetzt kleinere Portionen. → **We now eat smaller portions.**

a Sie isst ein gesünderes Frühstück als vorher.

....

b Die frischere Luft in den Bergen ist gut für Lungenkranke.

....

c Meine Freundin hat eine bessere Ernährung als ich.

....

d Mein Vater hat einen stressigeren Beruf als meine Mutter.

....

e Die süßeren Getränke sind nicht so gesund wie Wasser.

....

B Modal verbs *müssen* and *dürfen*

STUDENT BOOK 9.2 **GRAMMAR SECTION** F1

> *Müssen* and *dürfen* are two of the six modal verbs. They are used in combination with another verb in the infinitive to say what you must do (*müssen*) and what you are allowed to do (*dürfen*):
>
> *Ich **muss** mir die Hände waschen.*
> I must wash my hands.
>
> *Wir **dürfen** spät aufstehen.*
> We are allowed to/may get up late.

müssen	
ich muss	wir müssen
du musst	ihr müsst
er/sie/es/man muss	Sie/sie müssen

dürfen	
ich darf	wir dürfen
du darfst	ihr dürft
er/sie/es/man darf	Sie/sie dürfen

There are different ways of expressing the meaning of these verbs in English. You might use 'have to' or 'has to' as well as 'must' for *müssen*, and 'may' or 'can' as well as 'is/are allowed to' for *dürfen*.

Take great care when looking at negative forms of *müssen*. *Du* **musst nicht** *zu Fuß gehen* means 'You don't have to walk' (suggesting that you can if you want to). If you want to forbid someone from doing something, you have to use *dürfen*:

Du **darfst nicht** *rauchen.*

You must not smoke.

3 These statements have been taken from a leaflet giving advice. Translate the extract into English. Start like this: 'You must eat healthily! You…'.

Du musst gesund essen! Du musst nicht nur Obst und Gemüse essen. Ab und zu darfst du auch Pommes oder Schokolade haben. Es darf aber nicht jeden Tag sein! Du darfst nicht zu spät ins Bett gehen. Am Abend musst du nicht immer die gleiche Routine haben, aber du musst versuchen, nicht zu spät zu essen.

....
....
....
....
....
....
....
....
....
....
....
....

4 Insert the correct form of the modal verb shown in brackets into the gaps.

e.g. Das Kind .... allein zur Schule laufen. (*dürfen*) → Das Kind **darf** allein zur Schule laufen.

a Ihr .... euch die Hände waschen. (*müssen*)

b Ich glaube, du .... zum Arzt gehen. (*müssen*)

c Wir .... bis Mitternacht ausbleiben. (*dürfen*)

d Alle Schüler .... Sport treiben. (*müssen*)

e Franz .... mehr Wasser trinken. (*müssen*)

f .... ihr so viel Salz essen? (*dürfen*)

g Warum .... Sie ins Krankenhaus gehen? (*müssen*)

C *Seit* and *schon* with present tense

Seit means 'for' or 'since'. If the situation that is being talked about is still going on, the present tense is used in German (whereas the past tense is used in English). If it is followed by a noun, the dative case must be used. *Schon* means 'already'.

Wie lange sind Sie **schon** *krank?*

How long have you (already) been ill?

Ich bin **seit** *ein***er** *Woche krank.*

I have been ill for a week.

Ich bin **seit** *letzt***em** *Monat krank.*

I have been ill since last month.

5 Anke doesn't feel well and doesn't want to go to school. Read this conversation between Anke and her mother and delete the words which are grammatically incorrect. The first has been done for you.

Mutter Wie lange ~~geht~~/~~ging~~/~~war~~ es dir schon schlecht?

Anke Also, seit gestern hatte/habe/haben ich Kopfschmerzen, aber mein Magen tut/tun/tat schon seit letzte/letzter/letztem Woche weh. Halsweh habe ich auch.

Mutter Seit wann haben/hattest/hast du schon Halsweh?

Anke Erst seit einige/einigen/einiger Stunden. In meinen Augen habe ich auch Schmerzen.

Mutter Seit wann tun/tut/tat dir die Augen weh?

Anke Seit meinen/meiner/meinem letzten Termin beim Augenarzt. Ich glaube, ich brauche eine neue Brille. Seit letzten/letzter/letztem Montag kann ich die Tafel nicht mehr sehen.

Mutter Komm, wir gehen sofort zum Arzt!

D Impersonal verbs with the dative

If you are saying something about yourself using an impersonal verb, the subject is not *ich*. Instead, you need to use the dative form of *ich*, which is *mir*:

Mir geht's schlecht.

I don't feel well (Literally: 'It goes badly to me.')

Ihm ist schwindelig.

He is dizzy (Literally: 'It is dizzy to him.')

Geht's Ihnen gut?

Are you well?

This construction is useful for talking about aches and pains using the separable verb *wehtun*:

Mein Magen tut mir weh.

My stomach hurts.

Meine Augen tun mir weh.

My eyes hurt.

Be careful to use the singular (*tut*) or plural (*tun*) part of the verb depending on what is hurting. You can use this verb without the dative pronoun, because it is clear who is experiencing the pain:

Mein Ohr tut (mir) weh.

My ear hurts (me).

Meine Ohren tun (mir) weh.

My ears hurt (me).

Pronouns in the dative:

Nom	Dat	Nom	Dat
ich	mir	wir	uns
du	dir	ihr	euch
er	ihm	Sie	Ihnen
sie	ihr	sie	ihnen
es	ihm		

6 Insert the dative pronoun or the correct form of the verb *wehtun* in each sentence.

e.g. Frau Klein hat Kopfschmerzen. Der Kopf .... weh. → Der Kopf **tut ihr** weh.

a Wir sind wieder gesund. .... geht's gut.

b Mein Sohn hat Fieber. .... ist heiß.

c Sie haben Kopfschmerzen. Ist .... auch schwindelig?

d Meine Beine .... weh.

e Meine Schwester ist krank. .... geht's schlecht.

f Ich habe Halsweh und .... ist kalt.

g Sein Kopf .... weh.

h Ihr hattet Durchfall. Geht's .... jetzt besser?

i Die Kinder sind umgefallen. .... war schwindelig.

E Dative reflexive pronouns

When you talk about a broken arm or leg you need to use the accusative for the limb (e.g. *den Arm*) and the dative for the pronouns *mir* and *dir*. However, the other pronouns (*sich, uns, euch*) are the same as those used with reflexive verbs:

Ich habe mir das Bein gebrochen.

I have broken my leg.

Sie hat sich den Arm gebrochen.

She has broken her arm.

7 These statements were overheard at a fracture clinic. Complete the sentences as in the example.

e.g. Karls Ellbogen tut weh. Er ....

→ Karls Ellbogen tut weh. Er **hat sich den Ellbogen gebrochen**.

a Susis Rücken tut weh.

Sie ....

b Mein Fuß tut mir weh.

Ich ....

c Dein Knie tut weh.

Du ....

d Eure Beine tun weh.

Ihr ....

e Unsere Nasen tun weh.

Wir ....

F The passive voice

> The passive voice is used when the subject of the verb is not carrying out the action, but is on the receiving end of it. This sentence is passive:
>
> *Die Patienten **werden** ins Krankenhaus **gebracht**.*
>
> The patients are brought into the hospital.
>
> *Werden* is used to form the passive, along with a past participle. Here, it is not reflecting a future tense. The passive can be used in any tense by changing the tense of *werden*.

8 This paragraph is part of a report about an accident and contains a number of verbs in the passive. Translate it into English. Start like this: 'The car was driven by a young woman.'

> Das Auto wurde von einer jungen Frau gefahren. Ein Kind wurde schwer verletzt. Der Unfall wurde von vielen Menschen gesehen. Ein Krankenwagen wurde sofort gerufen. Das Kind wurde schnell ins Krankenhaus gebracht. Die Eltern wurden informiert. Das Kind wird jetzt im Krankenhaus betreut.

betreuen = to care for

....
....
....
....
....
....
....
....
....

> The passive voice is less common in German than in English. A common way of avoiding the passive is the use of the pronoun *man* (someone):
>
> ***Man** passt auf die Verletzten auf.*
>
> The injured people are looked after.
> (Literally: 'Someone looks after the injured.')

9 Rewrite the passive sentences (from a report about an accident) using *man*. Use the perfect tense.

e.g. Das Auto wurde zu schnell gefahren. → **Man hat das Auto zu schnell gefahren.**

a Das schwarze Auto wurde nicht gesehen, weil es dunkel war.

....
....
....

b Die Polizei wurde alarmiert.

....
....
....

c Der Hubschrauber wurde gerufen.

....
....
....

d Der Fahrer und die Passagiere wurden ins Krankenhaus gebracht.

....
....
....

e Das kaputte Auto wurde weggebracht.

....
....
....

f Die Verletzten wurden im Krankenhaus besucht.

....
....
....

Thema 10 Meine Stadt und meine Gegend

A Personal pronouns

German pronouns change according to their case.

Nom	Acc	Dat
ich	mich	mir
du	dich	dir
er	ihn	ihm
sie	sie	ihr
es	es	ihm
wir	uns	uns
ihr	euch	euch
Sie	Sie	Ihnen
sie	sie	ihnen

Subject pronouns are used instead of the subject of the verb, when you already know what that subject is. They are therefore always in the **nominative** case:

Ich wohne in München.

I live in Munich.

Personal pronouns can be in the **accusative** case for two reasons:
- When they are used instead of the direct object of the verb, when you already know who or what is being referred to:

Meine Nachbarn kennen mich.

My neighbours know me.

- Following prepositions that take the **accusative**:

Ich habe etwas für dich.

I have something for you.

Pronouns are used in the **dative** case:
- When they replace the indirect object of the verb when you already know who or what is being indirectly referred to:

Ich gebe dir ein Geschenk.

I give you a present.

- Following prepositions that take the dative:

Meine Schwester geht mit mir in die Stadt.

My sister goes into town with me.

1. Fill the gap with an accusative pronoun. Look at the word(s) in bold to help you select the correct one.

   e.g. Man kauft dieses Haus für **meine Mutter**. Es ist für .... → Es ist für **sie**.

   a **Sie** findet **das Haus** schön. Sie mag ....

   b **Der Garten** ist auch schön. Sie mag .... auch.

   c Der Garten hat **einen großen Baum**. Siehst du .... ?

   d **Wir** wohnen am Stadtrand. Besuchst du .... dort?

   e **Du** wohnst jetzt in einem Dorf. Hat das Vorteile für .... ?

   f **Ihr** lebt neben einem Restaurant. Ist das zu laut für .... ?

   g **Ich** wohne weit vom Stadtzentrum. Am Abend gehen meine Freunde oft ohne .... aus.

2. Fill the gap with a dative pronoun. Look at the word(s) in bold to help you select the correct one.

   e.g. Hajo wohnt bei **seiner Tante**. Er wohnt seit einem Jahr bei .... → Er wohnt seit einem Jahr bei **ihr**.

   a **Meine Großeltern** haben ihr Haus gebaut. Es wurde von .... gebaut.

   b Ich fahre mit **meinem Freund** in die Stadtmitte. Ich fahre mit .... dorthin.

   c **Ich** komme später mit meinem Freund zurück. Er kommt mit .... zurück.

   d **Wir** wohnen gegenüber unserem Lehrer. Der Lehrer wohnt .... gegenüber.

   e Wer wohnt noch **in Ihrem Haus**? Wer wohnt noch bei .... ?

   f **Ihr** habt uns besucht. Das nächste Mal kommen wir zu ....

   g **Meine Freundin Angelika** wohnt nebenan. Ich kann mit .... zur Schule fahren.

3. Answer the questions using pronouns, as in the example. There will be two pronouns in each answer and you need to decide if they are in the nominative, accusative or dative case.

   e.g. Hast du den Dom besucht? → **Ja, ich habe ihn besucht.**

   a Ist der Bahnhof neben dem Park?

   Ja, ...

   b Findet ihr euer Dorf schön?

   Ja, ...

   c Liegt die Stadt weit vom Strand entfernt?

   Ja, ...

d Müssen Sie durch die Stadtmitte fahren?

Ja, ...

e Kennst du Menschen außer deinen Verwandten hier?

Ja, ...

B The verb *gefallen*

STUDENT BOOK 10.2 — GRAMMAR SECTION G1

> In German there are many ways to express likes and dislikes. One way is to use the impersonal verb *gefallen*. The person who likes or dislikes something needs to be in the dative case. The thing which is liked or disliked becomes the subject. For example, to say 'I like the town' you could say: *Ich mag die Stadt*. Using *gefallen* this becomes:
>
> *Die Stadt **gefällt mir**.*
>
> You could think of it as 'The town pleases me.' To express 'I like' with something in the plural, the verb *gefallen* has to agree with the plural subject:
>
> *Die Häuser **gefallen mir**.*
>
> I like the houses. (The houses please me.)

4 Here is a list of things which different people like and dislike about a town. Make up sentences for each line of the table as in the example. Check which pronouns to use in section A above.

Wer?	☺	☹
Sabine	der Dom	die Hochhäuser
a Herr Maier	das Kino	das Theater
b ich	der Fußballplatz	die Tennisplätze
c wir	der Jugendklub	die Schwimmhalle
d Herr und Frau Schwarz	die Cafés	die Restaurants
e Andreas	der Bahnhof	die Geschäfte
f ihr	das Zentrum	der Stadtrand
g Sie	das Dorf	die Stadt
h du	die Kirchen	das Schloss

e.g. **Der Dom gefällt ihr, aber die Hochhäuser gefallen ihr nicht.**

a ....

b ....

c ....

d ....

e ....

f ....

g ....

h ....

> The verb *gefallen* can be used in any tense. This is how it appears in the verb table:
>
> *gefallen   gefällt   gefiel   gefallen*

5 Translate these opinions about German towns using *gefallen* in the present tense, then rewrite each one in the tense shown in brackets.

e.g. We like Hamburg. (perfect) → **Hamburg gefällt uns. Hamburg hat uns gefallen.**

a She likes Dortmund. (future)

....

b They like Berlin. (imperfect)

....

c I don't like Bonn. (future)

....

d He likes Frankfurt and Mainz. (perfect)

....

e We don't like Kiel and Düsseldorf. (imperfect)

....

C Other verbs taking the dative

GRAMMAR SECTION A6

> The verb *gefallen* is not used if you are talking about liking or disliking food. The verb *schmecken* is used instead, but it works in the same way, with dative pronouns or other forms of the dative.
>
> *Käse **schmeckt mir**.*
>
> I like cheese.
>
> *Erbsen **schmecken meinem** Bruder nicht.*
>
> My brother doesn't like peas.

> Other useful verbs taking a dative are: *helfen* (to help), *folgen* (to follow), *gehören* (to belong to), *glauben* (to believe), *passen* (to fit), *reichen* (to be enough), *Leid tun* (to be sorry).

6 Match up the sentence beginnings (a–g) and endings (i–vii) and then translate the completed sentences into English.

a Ich kann heute nicht arbeiten und das…

b Frau Walter isst keine Wurst, denn Fleisch…

c Das ist nicht mein Hund, aber er…

d Unser Haus hat nur zwei Schlafzimmer und das…

e Die Party findet in der Wohnung statt, die…

f Ich habe zu viel zu tun, um…

g Du sagst, du hast deine eigene Wohnung, aber…

i …folgt mir immer nach Hause.

ii …tut mir Leid.

iii …dir zu helfen.

iv …ich glaube dir nicht.

v …reicht uns nicht mehr.

vi …meiner Freundin gehört.

vii …schmeckt ihr nicht.

a ……………………………………………………
b ……………………………………………………
c ……………………………………………………
d ……………………………………………………
e ……………………………………………………
f ……………………………………………………
g ……………………………………………………

D Indefinite pronouns

GRAMMAR SECTION **D6**

> Indefinite pronouns are used for more general or vague subjects than specific pronouns such as 'I' or 'he' are used for. Indefinite pronouns include:
>
> *jemand* (someone)
>
> *niemand* (nobody)
>
> *etwas* (something)
>
> *nichts* (nothing)
>
> *man* (one, you, referring to people generally)
>
> *Jemand wohnt hier, aber ich weiß nicht wer.*
>
> Someone lives here, but I don't know who.
>
> *Nichts ist unmöglich.*
>
> Nothing is impossible.

7 Insert a different indefinite pronoun from the list above into each gap. The first gap has been filled for you.

> Meine Stadt ist fantastisch. Sie hat etwas für alle: Sportmöglichkeiten, ein Kino, ein Theater, tolle Geschäfte… Hier langweilt sich ……………………… Ich gehe gern in den Park, wo ……………………… Rad fahren oder spazieren gehen kann. Vor zwei Tagen hat mir ……………………… gesagt: „Hier ist es langweilig. Es gibt ……………………… zu tun", aber das verstehe ich nicht. Es ist die beste Stadt der Welt!

Thema 11 Einkaufen und so weiter

A Asking questions using 'Was für...?'

Was für (*ein*) is used to ask 'what?' or 'what sort of?'. *Was für* should be used in the same way as any other question word (e.g. *wann?*, *wo?*) even though it is actually two words.

While the second part is '*für*', this is not used as a preposition here and so should not necessarily be followed by the accusative. When *was für* is followed by *ein*, *ein* will change its form according to the case and gender of the noun being used. The case will depend on how the noun is used in the sentence:

Was für ein Geschäft ist das? (*Geschäft* is the subject, so nominative)

What sort of shop is that?

Was für einen Rock möchten Sie? (*Rock* is the direct object, so accusative)

What sort of skirt would you like?

1 Write out questions beginning with *was für* which could result in the answers below.

e.g. **Was für ein Auto ist das?**

Das ist ein Porsche.

a Was für ....

Ich habe eine blaue Hose gekauft.

b ....

Ich mag schwarze Schuhe.

c ....

Er möchte einen warmen Mantel.

d ....

Sie sucht die Größe 40.

e ....

Die Kinder kaufen ein großes Eis.

B Forming questions using 'Welcher...?'

Welcher means 'which' and is an interrogative adjective. 'Interrogative' means that it is used for asking questions, and the fact that it is an adjective means that its ending changes according to number, gender and case. The endings are the same as for the definite article (*der, die, das*):

	m	f	n	pl
Nom	welcher	welche	welches	welche
Acc	welchen	welche	welches	welche
Gen	welches	welcher	welches	welcher
Dat	welchem	welcher	welchem	welchen

Welches Hemd ist zu groß?

Which shirt is too big?

Welchen Rock wird sie kaufen?

Which skirt will she buy?

2 Which form of *welcher* is correct in these questions? Delete the ones that are wrong.

e.g. ~~Welches~~/**welche**/~~welchen~~ Größe ist dieser Pullover?

a Welcher/welches/welchen Mantel passt dir?

b Welcher/welches/welchen Mantel kaufst du?

c Welche/welcher/welchen Kleider gefallen dir?

d Welche/welches/welchen Kleid ist das Schönste?

e In welcher/welchem/welchen Geschäft hast du das gekauft?

f Aus welcher/welchem/welchen Umkleidekabine kam diese Frau?

g Für welche/welcher/welchem Party ist das Kleid?

h An welchen/welcher/welchem Tag wirst du es kaufen?

C Demonstrative adjectives and pronouns: *dieser* and *jener*

Dieser corresponds to the English 'this', or 'these' in the plural. *Jener* is 'that', or 'those' in the plural. The endings on both *dieser* and *jener* change in the same way as the definite article *der, die, das*, i.e. in the same way as *welcher* in the table above.

Dieser Pullover ist schön.

This sweater is nice.

Ich mag *diesen* Pullover.

I like this sweater.

If you use 'this' and 'that' to compare two similar things, you don't need to repeat the noun:

Diese Bluse ist zu klein, aber *jene* kostet viel.

This blouse is too small but **that one** costs a lot.

In this case *jene* is a pronoun but its ending is the same as if the noun *Bluse* were following it.

3 Match up the beginnings (a–g) and endings (i–vii) of these sentences. Look carefully at the endings on *dieser* and *jener*. The gender needs to be the same as in the first half, although the case might change.

a Dieses Kleid ist zu alt, aber…
b Diese Kleider sind modern, aber…
c In dieses Geschäft gehe ich gern, aber…
d Diesen Rock finde ich schön, aber…
e Für diese Schuhe würde ich viel Geld ausgeben, aber…
f Dieser dunkle Mantel gefällt mir besser, weil…
g Diese Größe passt mir gut, aber…

i …in jenem gibt es nichts für mich.
ii …für jene zahle ich nichts.
iii …jene ist zu eng.
iv …jene sind altmodisch.
v …jener zu hell ist.
vi …jenen mag ich nicht.
vii …jenes passt mir nicht.

4 For each of the sentences you made in exercise 3, write down which case and gender (or plural) was used for each form of *dieser* and *jener*. The first has been done for you.

a *dieses* – **nominative, neuter**; *jenes* – **nominative, neuter**
b *diese* – ....
c ....
d ....
e ....
f ....
g ....

D Relative pronouns

STUDENT BOOK 11.2 GRAMMAR SECTION D4

> Relative pronouns in English are 'who', 'that' and 'which' when these words are used in the context of linking two sentences, such as:
>
> This is the computer. It costs 400 euros. →
> This is the computer **which** costs 400 Euros.
>
> The lady is called Frau Müller. She works in the shop. → The lady **who** works in the shop is called Frau Müller.
>
> In German, relative pronouns introduce a relative clause where, as in all subordinate clauses, the verb goes to the end:
>
> *Hier ist der Computer, **der** 400 Euro **kostet**.*
>
> *Die Frau, **die** im Geschäft **arbeitet**, heißt Frau Müller.*

> Relative pronouns agree in number (singular/plural) and gender with the noun to which they refer (*der Computer, der…*; *die Frau, die…*). In these examples both the nouns and the relative pronouns are nominative. In later examples you will see how the case of the relative pronoun can change from the case of the noun it relates to.

5 Insert the correct relative pronoun into the gap. It will be in the nominative case, but check back to see which gender and number (singular or plural) are needed. Translate the sentences into English.

e.g. Hier ist das Geschäft, ... ganz neu ist. → Hier ist das Geschäft, **das** ganz neu ist. → **Here is the shop which is quite new.**

a Wo ist die Hose, ... so billig war?
....
....

b Hier sind die Kleider, ... sehr modern sind.
....
....

c Mein Bruder, ... als Verkäufer arbeitet, hat eine neue Stelle.
....
....

d Das T-Shirt, ... im Angebot ist, ist toll.
....
....

e Das ist der Mann, ... im Supermarkt arbeitet.
....
....

> The grammatical case of the relative pronoun depends on its role within the relative clause.
>
> *Hier ist der Mann, **den** ich kenne.*
>
> Here is the man who/whom I know.
>
> In this example, the relative pronoun *den* is the same gender and number (i.e. singular) as in the main clause (*der Mann*), but its case has changed as it is the direct object in the relative clause, just as it would be if the two sentences were separate:
>
> *Hier ist der Mann. Ich kenne **ihn**.*
>
> In English it is possible to miss out the relative clause: 'Here is the man I know' but you can't do this in German.
>
> This is the table showing relative pronouns in different genders and cases:
>
> | | m | f | n | pl |
> |-----|------|------|--------|-------|
> | Nom | der | die | das | die |
> | Acc | den | die | das | die |
> | Gen | dessen | deren | dessen | deren |
> | Dat | dem | der | dem | denen |

> Sometimes the relative pronoun will be used along with a preposition:
>
> *Silke ist die Freundin, **mit der** ich einkaufen gehe.*
>
> Silke is the friend with whom I go shopping.
>
> The relative pronoun *der* is in the dative following the preposition *mit*. Note that in current English we might say 'Silke is the friend I go shopping with' but in German you must put the preposition before the relative clause, as in the example shown.
>
> The genitive is used to express 'whose':
>
> *Das ist die Frau, **deren** Mann im Schuhgeschäft arbeitet.*
>
> That is the woman whose husband works in the shoe shop.
>
> In this case, the relative pronoun is feminine because it relates back to the woman.

6 Choose which relative pronouns are correct in this text about a shopping trip. Delete those which are not correct, as in the first sentence.

> Hier ist das Bild, **das/der/dem** ich für meinen Vater gekauft habe. Mein Vater, **deren/dem/dessen** Geburtstag heute ist, freut sich sehr. Das Geschäft, in **der/das/dem** ich es gekaufte habe, ist in der Stadtmitte. In einem anderen Geschäft, **das/der/dessen** gegenüber dem Bahnhof liegt, habe ich schöne Handschuhe gekauft. Die Handschuhe, **der/die/deren** aus Leder sind, sind für meine Mutter. Ich habe einen Freund, **den/der/das** jetzt im Krankenhaus ist. Für ihn habe ich zwei Bücher gekauft. Dieser Freund, **den/der/dem** ich seit Jahren schon kenne, hat sich das Bein gebrochen. Die Bücher, **deren/die/das** ich ihm schenken werde, sind Krimis. Meine Schwester, mit **die/der/dem** ich im Einkaufszentrum war, hat auch Geschenke gekauft. Unsere Eltern, mit **der/dem/denen** wir uns gut verstehen, haben uns in letzter Zeit sehr geholfen und wir wollten ihnen „Danke schön" sagen.

7 Rewrite each pair of sentences as one sentence containing a relative clause. The relative pronoun will be the same gender/number and in the same case as the pronoun in bold in the second of each pair of sentences.

e.g. Sie kauft den Rock. **Er** ist billig. → **Sie kauft den Rock, der billig ist.**

a Sie mag das Kleid. **Es** ist nicht sehr modisch.

b Wie findest du die Hose? Ich kaufte **sie**.

c Hier sind die CDs. Du suchst **sie**.

d Ich möchte die Tasche. **Sie** kostet zwanzig Euro.

e Wo ist der Mantel? Du hast **ihn** gestern gekauft.

f Wir mögen die Sachen. Es gibt **sie** in diesem Geschäft.

g Ich kaufe nur Kleider. **Sie** werden auch nächstes Jahr passen.

> *Was* is also used as a relative pronoun, but unlike the above, it does not change according to gender, number or case. It is used mainly after *alles* and *nichts*.
>
> *Alles, **was** ich anprobiere, passt mir nicht.*
>
> Everything I try on doesn't fit me.
>
> *Nichts, **was** ich anprobiere, passt mir.*
>
> Nothing I try on fits me.

8 Insert the correct relative pronoun into each gap. Be careful; there are examples from all the cases.

e.g. Patricia mag die Geburtstagsgeschenke, ... sie bekommt. → Patricia mag die Geburtstagsgeschenke, **die** sie bekommt.

a Ich habe einen reichen Freund, ... immer ein neues Handy hat.

b Wo ist das Mädchen, ... Tasche hier ist?

c Der Junge, für .... ich diesen Fußball kaufe, ist mein Bruder.

d Meine Freundin hat viel Geld. Sie kauft alles, ... sie will.

e Dort sind die Kaufhäuser, in .... ich sehr gern einkaufe.

f Nichts, ... ich sehe, gefällt mir.

g Ich mag alles, ... modern ist!

Thema 12 Essen und Trinken

A Plural forms of nouns (revision)

When you learn a new noun, learn the singular and plural forms together. German nouns form their plurals in lots of different ways.

Masculine nouns tend to add an *-e* (where appropriate, there is also an umlaut):

> der Fisch → die Fisch**e**
> der Supermarkt → die Superm**ä**rkt**e**

Masculine nouns that end in *-el*, *-en* or *-er* may not change in the plural:

> der Becher → die Becher

but some may take an Umlaut:

> der Apfel → die **Ä**pfel

Feminine nouns tend to add an *-n* or *-en*:

> die Banane → die Banane**n**
> die Karotte → die Karotte**n**

Neuter nouns tend to add *-e* or *-er* (where appropriate, there is also an umlaut):

> das Getränk → die Getränk**e**   das Ei → die Ei**er**
> das Glas → die Gl**ä**s**er**

The ending *-s* is only used to form plurals of nouns taken from another language:

> das Steak → die Steak**s**
> das Restaurant → die Restaurant**s**

Compound nouns take their plural from the last element in the word:

> die Suppe → die Suppe**n**, therefore
> die Gemüsesuppe → die Gemüsesuppe**n**

Note that there are many exceptions to these rules so it is always best to check in a glossary or dictionary.

1 Write the English meanings and the plural forms of these nouns. Check them in a dictionary!

e.g. das Käsebrot   cheese sandwich   die Käsebrote

a die Torte ....
b der Fisch ....
c die Erbsensuppe ....
d der Kuchen ....
e die Wurst ....
f das Hähnchen ....
g die Nuss ....
h das Kotelett ....
i der Kartoffelsalat ....

2 What is the singular of these plural nouns? Include the definite article and the meaning.

e.g. die Gurken   die Gurke   cucumber

a die Würstchen ....
b die Gemüse ....
c die Spiegeleier ....
d die Schnitzel ....
e die Zwiebeln ....
f die Bohnen ....
g die Fruchtsäfte ....
h die Kartoffeln ....
i die Apfelsinen ....

B Adjective endings in nominative and accusative (revision)

When adjectives are placed before a noun their endings change according to gender, case and number (singular or plural), but also depending on whether they follow the definite or indefinite article, or no article at all. These tables show the nominative and accusative adjective endings to be used after the definite and indefinite article.

	m	f	n	pl
Nom	der rot**e** Apfel	die gelb**e** Banane	das weiß**e** Ei	die grün**en** Birnen
Acc	den rot**en** Apfel	die gelb**e** Banane	das weiß**e** Ei	die grün**en** Birnen

Following the definite article, it is only in the masculine that the accusative ending is different from the nominative.

	m	f	n	pl
Nom	ein rot**er** Apfel	eine gelb**e** Banane	ein weiß**es** Ei	keine grün**en** Birnen
Acc	einen rot**en** Apfel	eine gelb**e** Banane	ein weiß**es** Ei	keine grün**en** Birnen

As with the definite article, it is in the masculine form where the nominative and accusative are different. Note that in the nominative case the masculine and neuter indefinite article are the same (*ein*). The gender of the noun can be seen from the adjective ending (*ein roter* — masculine; *ein rotes* — neuter). The indefinite article endings are also used following possessive adjectives (*mein*, *dein* etc.) and the negative word *kein*.

3 Insert the correct endings on to the adjectives in this short text about shopping. The first has been done for you.

> Ich habe vor, ein tolles Abendessen für meine best........ Freunde zu kochen. Ich gehe in den neu....... Supermarkt um die Ecke. Für das lecker....... Hauptgericht brauche ich ein groß....... Stück Fleisch, ein halb....... Kilo Kartoffeln, eine klein....... Dose Oliven und einen grün....... Kopfsalat. Nachher werde ich zum Markt gehen, wo man die best....... Tomaten bekommt. Das frisch....... Obst für den Nachtisch werde ich dort auch kaufen. Dazu werden wir ein gemischt....... Eis essen.

C Using *gern/lieber/am liebsten*

> Use *gern* (or *nicht gern*) to say you do (or don't) like doing something. It is an adverb that can be used with any verb and its ending doesn't change:
>
> *Ich esse **gern** Käse.*
> I like eating cheese.
>
> *Er isst **nicht gern** Gemüse.*
> He doesn't like eating vegetables.
>
> The comparative and superlative forms of *gern* are *lieber* and *am liebsten*:
>
> *Ich esse **gern** Fisch, aber ich esse **lieber** Hähnchen.*
> I like to eat fish but I prefer to eat chicken.
>
> *Ich esse **am liebsten** Wurst.*
> I like eating sausage best.

4 Three friends with different tastes go out to eat. These are the menus from three restaurants. Which one do they choose to go to? Write A, B or C.

A	B	C
Fischsuppe	Bunter Salat	Eiersalat
Bratwurst mit Brot oder Kartoffelsalat	Lachs mit Salzkartoffeln oder Pommes	Hähnchen mit Erbsen, Pommes oder Reis
Käsekuchen	Torte oder Käse	Eis mit Sahne

Alex isst gern Fisch, aber er isst lieber Hähnchen. Er isst nicht gern Eier. Am liebsten isst er Süßes. ....

Bernd isst gern Gemüse, aber er isst lieber Salat. Käse isst er überhaupt nicht gern. Er isst lieber Fleisch oder Fisch. Kartoffeln isst er lieber als Reis. ....

Kristian isst nicht gern Süßes. Er isst am liebsten Pommes. Würstchen isst er gern, aber Hähnchen und Fisch isst er lieber. ....

5 Write sentences as in the example.

e.g. Brot/Kekse/Kuchen (*ich – essen*) → Ich esse gern Brot, aber ich esse lieber Kekse. Ich esse am liebsten Kuchen.

a Erbsen/Karotten/Kartoffeln (*mein Bruder – essen*)

....
....
....
....
....

b Orangensaft/Milch/Cola (*wir – trinken*)

....
....
....
....
....

c Wasser/Tee/Kaffee (*meine Mutter – trinken*)

....
....
....
....
....

D The verb *schmecken* (revision)

> Another way of saying that you like or dislike the taste of food and drink is to use the impersonal verb *schmecken*. The person who likes or dislikes something needs to be in the dative case, while the food is in the nominative. The verb will be in the third person singular (*schmeckt*) for a singular item of food or drink, and in the third person plural (*schmecken*) for a plural item.
>
> *Der Kuchen **schmeckt mir**.*
> I like the cake.
>
> *Eier **schmecken ihm** nicht.*
> He doesn't like eggs.
>
> You can add adverbs such as *gut, besser, gar nicht* to emphasise how much something is liked or disliked.
>
> *Käsekuchen **schmeckt mir gut**, aber Schokoladenkuchen **schmeckt mir am besten**.*
> I really like cheese cake, but I like chocolate cake best.
>
> Here is a reminder of the dative pronouns:

Nom	Dat
ich	mir
du	dir
er	ihm
sie	ihr
es	ihm
wir	uns
ihr	euch
Sie	Ihnen
sie	ihnen

6 Use the words in the box to create a German version of the sentences below. The first has been started for you.

Apfelsinen	~~schmeckt~~	gar nicht	ihm
Tee	uns	ihr	schmeckt
schmeckt	schmecken	besser als	aber
ihnen	gut	Kaffee	
nicht	~~Käse~~	Bananen	

a We don't like cheese at all.

Käse schmeckt ....
....
....

b She likes oranges better than bananas.

....
....
....

c They like coffee but he doesn't like tea.

....
....
....

E Strong (irregular) verbs in the present tense

STUDENT BOOK **12.3** GRAMMAR SECTION **F1**

Some verbs that have an 'e' in the stem (e.g. *geben, nehmen, essen*) change the vowel to an 'i' in the second and third person singular in the present tense.

essen (to eat)	
ich esse	wir essen
du isst	ihr esst
er/sie/es/man isst	Sie/sie essen

7 Insert the correct form of the verb in brackets in the gap.

e.g. Was .... du als Vorspeise? (*nehmen*) → Was **nimmst** du als Vorspeise?

a Meine Katze .... gern Fisch. (*fressen*)

b Ich werde zahlen, wenn du mir das Geld .... (*geben*)

c Herr Friedrich .... immer, dass er Diät macht. (*vergessen*)

d An deinem Geburtstag .... du von mir einen Kuchen bekommen. (*werden*)

e Andrea .... immer zu viel, wenn sie .... (*sprechen, essen*)

f Mein Vater .... mich ins teuere Restaurant mit. (*nehmen*)

F Subordinating conjunctions (revision): *damit, so dass, bevor, nachdem*

STUDENT BOOK **12.4** GRAMMAR SECTION **H4**

Subordinating conjunctions introduce a subordinate clause and send the verb to the end of the clause. Subordinating conjunctions you have already met include *weil* (because), *obwohl* (although), *da* (since), *wenn* (when, if). Here are some more useful conjunctions:

- *damit* (in order that):

  *Man soll viel Wasser trinken, **damit** man gesund bleibt.*

  You should drink lots of water in order to stay healthy.

- *so dass* (as a result):

  *Er hat viel Wasser getrunken, **so dass** er jetzt sehr gesund ist.*

  He drank lots of water and as a result he is very healthy.

- *bevor* (before):

  *Ich esse wenig, **bevor** ich Sport treibe.*

  I don't eat much before I do sport.

- *nachdem* (after):

  *Man soll Wasser trinken, **nachdem** man Sport getrieben hat.*

  You should drink water after you have done sport.

A subordinate clause can come at the beginning of the sentence, in which case the main verb comes directly after the comma which separates the clauses, giving the pattern: verb–comma–verb:

***Damit** man gesund **bleibt**, **soll** man viel Wasser trinken.*

8 Link up the beginnings (a–f) and endings (i–vi) of the sentences.

a Man muss sich die Hände waschen, bevor…

b Damit wir keinen Hunger haben,…

c Ich habe immer viele Vitaminen gegessen, so dass…

d Das Kind darf Nachtisch essen, nachdem…

e Bevor ich frühstücke,…

f Nachdem du gegessen hast,…

i …gibt man uns ein Brot zum mitnehmen.

ii …es Gemüse gegessen hat.

iii …koche ich Kaffee.

iv …musst du abwaschen.

v …man das Essen vorbereitet.

vi …ich selten krank bin.

9 These jumbled sentences each contain a subordinate clause. Rewrite each one twice, once beginning with the subordinate clause and once ending with it. You will need to add punctuation.

e.g. wenig essen nicht wird man dick soll damit Fett man →

Man soll wenig Fett essen, damit man nicht dick wird.

Damit man nicht dick wird, soll man wenig Fett essen.

a Gemüse wir machen die wir bevor müssen die schneiden Suppe

....

....

....

....

....

b wir die kochen gekauft Lebensmittel nachdem werden wir haben

....

....

....

....

....

Thema 13 Medien

A Imperfect tense

STUDENT BOOK **13.2** | GRAMMAR SECTION **F4**

The imperfect tense, like the perfect tense, is used to describe past events or situations that are now finished. There are no rules telling you whether to use the imperfect or the perfect, but the imperfect is used more frequently in written texts. Verbs can be regular (weak) such as *machen*, or irregular (strong) such as *gehen*. Mixed verbs have regular endings, but a different stem from the present tense (e.g. *denken*).

machen (to do – weak)	
ich machte	wir machten
du machtest	ihr machtet
er/sie/es/man machte	Sie/sie machten

gehen (to go – strong)	
ich ging	wir gingen
du gingst	ihr gingt
er/sie/es/man ging	Sie/sie gingen

denken (to think – mixed)	
ich dachte	wir dachten
du dachtest	ihr dachtet
er/sie/es/man dachte	Sie/sie dachten

1 You will need these verbs in exercise 2. Are they strong or weak? Tick the right box and then write the third person singular of the imperfect tense in the fourth column. You may need to check in the verb tables.

Infinitive	Strong or mixed	Weak	Third person
gehen	✓		ging
sehen			
spielen			
heißen			
reisen			
kommen			
wollen			
laufen			
haben			
wissen			
sollen			
müssen			
sein			
finden			

2 Insert the correct form of the verb in brackets in this film review. Remember to check the imperfect form of strong verbs in the verb table. The first verb has been done for you.

Gestern **ging** (*gehen*) ich mit meiner kleinen Schwester ins Kino. Wir .... (*sehen*) den Kinderfilm *Die Dinos sind los*. In diesem Film .... (*gehen*) es um drei Kinder, die mit einer Zeitmaschine .... (*spielen*). Die Jungen .... (*heißen*) Ernie und Max und das Mädchen .... (*heißen*)) Julia. Alle drei .... (*reisen*) in die Zeit der Dinosaurier zurück. Man .... (*kommen*) in einen Dschungel an. Ein Dinosaurier .... (*wollen*) die Kinder fressen, aber sie .... (*laufen*) immer fort. Die Kinder .... (*haben*) Angst, und .... (*wissen*) nicht, was sie tun .... (*sollen*). Jeder .... (*müssen*) den anderen helfen. Meiner Meinung nach .... (*sein*) der Film spannend für Kinder, aber ich .... (*finden*) es ein bisschen langweilig.

B Pluperfect tense

STUDENT BOOK **13.2** | GRAMMAR SECTION **F5**

The pluperfect expresses something that **had** happened before the event that is being talked about. To form the pluperfect tense, use the **imperfect** tense of *haben* or *sein* together with the relevant past participle. The rules about whether to use *haben* or *sein* are the same as for the perfect tense. Most verbs take *haben*. Verbs of motion, e.g. *gehen* and *fahren* (to go), and those which indicate a change of state, e.g. *sterben* (to die), take *sein*:

*Ich bin ins Kino gegangen, aber ich **hatte** den Film schon **gesehen**.*

I went to the cinema, but I had already seen the film.

*Elke ging um acht Uhr ins Restaurant, aber ihr Freund **war** eine halbe Stunde früher **angekommen**.*

Elke went to the restaurant at 8.00, but her boyfriend had arrived half an hour earlier.

3 All of these sentences describe a problem. The second clause should state that something had already happened. Finish the sentence using the word *schon* and the pluperfect of the verb in brackets, plus any other information given. Some of the verbs take *haben* and some take *sein*.

e.g. Ich wollte mit Anna ins Kino gehen, aber sie... (*den Film sehen*) → **hatte den Film schon gesehen.**

a Mein Freund schenkte mir ein Buch, aber ich... (*es lesen*)

....

....

b Wir sind um 7 Uhr am Theater angekommen, aber das Stück... (*anfangen*)

....

....

c Wir wollten mehr von der Gruppe hören, aber sie... (*zwei Stunden spielen*)

....

....

d Ich traf meine Freunde am Bahnhof, aber der Zug... (*abfahren*)

....

....

e Hannes kam etwas spät zum Konzert und sein Lieblingssänger... (*singen*)

....

....

f Meine Freundin hat mich gestern Abend angerufen, aber ich... (*ins Bett gehen*)

....

....

C Future tense (revision)

STUDENT BOOK **13.3** GRAMMAR SECTION **F6**

In German, as in English, the present tense is often used to express future ideas if a future time phrase is included:

*Ich fahre **nächste Woche** nach Berlin.*

I'm going to Berlin next week.

But there is also a future tense, formed using the correct form of the present tense of *werden* plus the infinitive of the relevant verb. This infinitive goes at the end of the sentence unless it is used in a subordinate clause:

*Ich **werde** ein neues Handy **kaufen**.*

I'm going to/I will buy a new mobile.

Ich spare mein Geld, weil ich ein neues Handy kaufen werde.

I'm saving my money because I'm going to buy a new mobile.

Here is the conjugation of *werden*. Note that on its own, *werden* means 'to become' but when used with another verb to form a future, it translates as 'will' or 'going to'.

werden	
ich werde	wir werden
du wirst	ihr werdet
er/sie/es/man wird	Sie/sie werden

4 All of these sentences are about something happening in the future. What do the sentences mean in English? Decide whether, in German, each one uses a future tense or a present tense with a future intention.

e.g. Wir werden im Internet chatten. → **We will chat on the internet.**

Future or present tense?
Future

a Die Schüler werden neue Computer bekommen.

....

....

b Nächste Woche kaufe ich ein neues E-Book.

....

....

c Wirst du das Internet bald zu Hause haben?

....

....

d Gerd wird in Zukunft keine Zeitungen mehr kaufen.

....

....

e Ab jetzt schreibe ich keine Briefe mehr!

....

....

f Gleich werden wir alle vergessen, wie man Briefe schreibt.

....

....

g Werden Sie viele E-mails schicken?

....

....

h Ich skype morgen meine Freundin in Norwegen.

....

....

5 How do these subordinate clauses finish? Choose the right ending.

a Meine Freundin wird sich freuen, dass ich ihr eine E-mail…
b Du musst Marco eine SMS schicken, damit er uns vor dem Theater…
c Weiß deine Mutter schon, dass wir Tickets für dieses Konzert…
d Weißt du schon, um wie viel Uhr du uns…
e Meine Freunde im Ausland haben mir gesagt, dass sie mir viele E-mails…
f Hast du das Buch gelesen, das ich morgen…

i …kaufen werden?
ii …schicken werden.
iii …schicken werde.
iv …treffen wirst?
v …kaufen werde?
vi …treffen wird.

D Summary of tenses

It is important that you can recognise different tenses. Here are examples of sentences in different tenses.

Present: *Er liest gern Romane.*
He likes reading novels.
Sie geht oft ins Kino.
She often goes to the cinema.

Imperfect: *Er las gern Romane.*
He liked reading novels.
Sie ging oft ins Kino.
She often went to the cinema.

Perfect: *Er hat gern Romane gelesen.*
He liked reading novels.
Sie ist oft ins Kino gegangen.
She often went to the cinema.

Pluperfect: *Er hatte gern Romane gelesen.*
He had liked reading novels.
Sie war oft ins Kino gegangen.
She had often gone to the cinema.

Future: *Er wird gern Romane lesen.*
He will like reading novels.
Sie wird oft ins Kino gehen.
She will often go to the cinema.

6 Read these sentences and identify which tense they are in by transferring the letter into the table below, as in the example.

Present	
Imperfect	
Perfect	a
Pluperfect	
Future	

a Wir sind in die Kirche gegangen, und haben das Bach-Konzert gehört.
b Um 8 Uhr begann die Filmaufführung.
c Wo hast du diese Informationen über das Theaterstück gefunden?
d Benutzt du oft Facebook?
e Die Schüler waren auch letztes Jahr im Ausland gefahren.
f Wir waren schon im Kino.
g Wann werdet ihr eure Fotos hochladen?
h Persönlich verschwende ich viel Zeit im Internet.
i Elke hatte das Buch schon zweimal gelesen.
j Endlich kam etwas Spannendes ins Kino!
k Der Lehrer hat uns vor den Gefahren des Internets gewarnt.
l Du musst aufhören, im Internet zu surfen.
m Hanna wird zum Geburtstag ein Smartphone bekommen.

E Adjectival endings after *etwas, nichts, viel, wenig, alles*

After these pronouns, adjectives are often used as neuter nouns and take a capital letter and endings. Here are some common examples:

Er liest etwas Interessantes.
He is reading something interesting.

In ihrer E-mail war nichts Wichtiges.
There was nothing important in her e-mail.

Note that after *etwas* (something), *nichts* (nothing), *viel* (much) and *wenig* (a little/few) the adjective endings are the same as those following the neuter indefinite article, but after *alles* (everything) you need to use the same endings as those following the neuter definite article:

Ich wünsche dir alles Gute.
I wish you all the best.

7 Choose the pronoun and adjectival noun from the box which best suit the meaning of this text. The first gap has been filled for you.

> viel Uninteressantes   nichts Besonderes
> alles Mögliche   wenig Nützliches
> etwas Lustiges   etwas Trauriges

Ich finde das Internet toll, weil man dort **alles Mögliche** finden kann. Heute habe ich viel im Internet gesurft, weil es Samstag ist und ich .... zu tun hatte. In den Nachrichten war leider .... über einen Autounfall. Aber dann habe ich auf einer anderen Webseite .... über meine Lieblingsshow im Fernsehen gelesen und ich musste sehr lachen. Mein Vater ist kein Internetfan. Er meint, es gibt .... und das stimmt auch. Wer möchte denn immer über Leute lesen, die man nicht kennt? Aber ich bin nicht seiner Meinung, dass es .... im Internet gibt, denn man kann oft Hilfe bekommen, wenn man etwas nicht versteht, oder man kann einkaufen oder Fahrkarten buchen.

Thema 14 Die Umwelt

A Impersonal verbs

Some weather expressions use impersonal verbs. This means they are normally only used in the *es* form, e.g. *schneien: es schneit* (it's snowing). The infinitives of other impersonal verbs are *regnen* (to rain), *frieren* (to freeze), *donnern* (to thunder) and *blitzen* (to flash with lightning).

1 Fill in the gaps in these tables to show how impersonal verbs can describe the weather in different tenses. Some have been done for you. Check in a verb table or a dictionary to see if they are regular or irregular.

schneien	
Present	
Imperfect	
Perfect	
Pluperfect	
Future	es wird schneien

regnen	
Present	es regnet
Imperfect	
Perfect	
Pluperfect	
Future	

frieren	
Present	
Imperfect	
Perfect	
Pluperfect	
Future	

donnern	
Present	
Imperfect	es donnerte
Perfect	
Pluperfect	
Future	

blitzen	
Present	
Imperfect	
Perfect	
Pluperfect	es hatte geblitzt
Future	

B The conditional

The conditional expresses the idea of 'would'. It is used to talk about actions that depend on certain conditions being fulfilled. The easiest way to express what you 'would do' is to use the conditional: combine the appropriate form of *würden* with the relevant infinitive (which goes at the end of the sentence):

Ich würde mehr Rad fahren. I would cycle more.

Würden is the **imperfect subjunctive** form of the verb *werden*:

ich würde	wir würden
du würdest	ihr würdet
er/sie/es/man würde	Sie/sie würden

2 Translate these sentences into German.

e.g. We would go on foot. → **Wir würden zu Fuß gehen.**

a She would recycle more.

....

....

b I would use solar energy.

....

....

c Would you (*du*) go by bus?

....

....

d He would buy a bike.

....

....

e They would save electricity.

....

....

f It would cost more.

....

....

g Anja and Heiko, would you go by bike?

....

....

For some common verbs, you do not need to use *würden*, as they have their own imperfect subjunctive forms. These have the same endings as *würden* (shown above), but the stem for each verb is irregular:

> Ich **wäre** vorsichtig. I would be careful.
>
> Ich **hätte** kein Auto. I would not have a car.
>
> Ich **könnte** mit dem Rad fahren. I could/would be able to travel by bike.
>
> Ich **möchte** mehr für die Umwelt tun. I would like to do more for the environment.
>
> Ich **sollte** mehr recyceln. I should recycle more.

The conditional is often used with the subordinating conjunction *wenn* (if):

> **Wenn** ich viel Zeit **hätte**, **würde** ich öfter zu Fuß **gehen**.
>
> If I had a lot of time I would walk more frequently.

Note that verbs in both parts of the sentence are in the conditional (...*hätte*, ...*würde*).

3 Fill in an appropriate verb in the conditional to match the meaning of the English sentences.

e.g. I could help more. Ich .... mehr helfen.
→ Ich **könnte** mehr helfen.

a You should shower.
Du .... duschen.

b We would be happier.
Wir .... glücklicher.

c They would like to help.
Sie .... helfen.

d Would you be able to walk?
.... Sie zu Fuß gehen?

e She could demonstrate.
Sie .... demonstrieren.

f I should use less electricity.
Ich .... weniger Strom benutzen.

g He would be able to have a bath.
Er .... baden.

h I would be annoyed.
Ich .... ärgerlich.

i You would have more time.
Ihr .... mehr Zeit.

j Would you like to do more?
.... du mehr tun?

4 Match up the sentence openings (a–f) and endings (i–vi).

a Wenn wir nicht so viele Autos hätten,…

b Wenn es keine Chemikalien im Meer geben würde,…

c Wenn es im Zentrum mehr Radwege geben würde,…

d Wenn man alternative Energiequellen benutzen würde,…

e Wenn alle Autos Elektroautos wären,…

f Wenn wir mehr recyceln würden,…

i …würden so viele Fische nicht sterben.

ii …wäre die Luft nicht so verschmutzt.

iii …würde man noch mehr Strom brauchen.

iv …hätten wir nicht so viel Müll.

v …würden wir öfter Rad fahren.

vi …würde es weniger Abgase geben.

5 Write out sentences b–f from exercise 4, switching around the main clause and the *wenn* clause as in the example.

e.g. **a** Es würde weniger Abgase geben, wenn wir nicht so viele Autos hätten.

b ....

c ....

d ....

e ....

f ....

C Comparative and superlative

STUDENT BOOK 14.4 GRAMMAR SECTION B8, B9

To compare two things you use the **comparative**, which is formed by adding *-er* to the adjective or adverb.

The **superlative** (highest, quickest etc.) is formed by using *am* and adding *-sten* or *-esten* to the adjective or adverb:

schlecht (bad)
schlechter (worse)
am schlechtesten (worst)

A preceding vowel (a, o, u) will take an umlaut in the comparative and superlative:

warm (warm)
wärmer (warmer)
am wärmsten (warmest)

In English, with longer adjectives, we often say 'more', e.g. 'more interesting'. In German this does not happen. You just add the endings:

interessant (interesting)
interessanter (more interesting)
am interessantesten (most interesting)

But note some exceptions:

viel (lots)	*mehr* (more)	*am meisten* (most)
gut (good)	*besser* (better)	*am besten* (best)
hoch (tall/high)	*höher* (taller/higher)	*am höchsten* (highest)

To say what you like doing, you can use the adverb *gern* with the verb. Its comparative and superlative forms are *lieber* and *am liebsten*:

*Ich fahre **gern** mit dem Bus.*
I like going by bus.

*Ich fahre **lieber** mit dem Zug.*
I prefer going by train.

*Ich fahre **am liebsten** mit dem Auto.*
I like going by car best.

Für mich ist die Umwelt sehr wichtig und ich liebe die Natur. Deutschland ist schön, aber Österreich finde ich <u>schöner</u>. Dort sind die Berge .... als im Nachbarland und das Wasser in den Seen ist oft .... als man denkt. Aber das Wasser ist nicht so warm wie das Mittelmeer, zum Beispiel an der Küste von Italien. Meine Mutter fährt viel .... an die Küste als in die Berge. Als ich .... war, fuhren wir oft im Urlaub nach Italien. Dann war das Wetter für uns am ...., aber jetzt gefällt es mir ...., wenn die Sonne nicht so heiß ist. In den großen italienischen Städten ist die Luftqualität .... als an der Küste. Und dort ist es auch immer so laut! Am .... ist es in Rom. Dort gibt es .... Autos als Menschen, glaube ich!

Comparative adjectives can also go in front of the noun and add endings in the same way as any other adjective:

*Mein Vater hat ein **schnelleres** Auto gekauft.*
My father has bought a faster car.

You can also place the superlative in front of the noun. In this case there is no *am* and you must add the correct adjective ending:

*Ich habe das billig**ste** Auto gekauft.*
I bought the cheapest car.

---

6 Insert a comparative or superlative adjective or adverb from the box into each gap. The first gap has been filled for you.

jünger	schlechter	~~schöner~~	besser
höher	lautesten	mehr	wärmer
wichtigsten	lieber		

7 Choose the correct form of the comparative or superlative adjectives by deleting the incorrect options.

e.g. Die ~~schlechtestes~~/~~schlechte~~/**schlechteste** Luft ist in den Großstädten.

a Das umweltfreundlichste/umweltfreundliche/umweltfreundlichstes Fahrzeug ist die Straßenbahn, oder?

b Die schnellste/schnellsten/schnellstes Autos haben die vielsten/mehren/meisten Abgase.

c Ältere/alten/altere Fahrzeuge sind umweltfeindlich.

d Windenergie ist eine moderne/modernere/modernerer Energiequelle als Gas.

e Ich habe den teurster/teuere/teuersten Wagen nicht gekauft.

8 How much do you know about Germany? Choose an adjective from the box and insert it in the appropriate place in its superlative form with the correct ending.

> windig   klein   groß   alt
> lang   tief   hoch   nördlich

e.g. Der .... Ort Deutschlands ist der Brocken im Harzgebirge. → Der **windigste** Ort Deutschlands ist der Brocken im Harzgebirge.

a Der .... Berg ist die Zugspitze.

b Der .... Fluss ist der Rhein.

c Das .... Bundesland ist Schleswig-Holstein.

d Die .... Stadt ist Berlin.

e Der .... See ist der Bodensee.

f Das .... Bundesland ist Bremen.

g Die .... Kirche ist in Trier.

Verb tables

* denotes verbs that take *sein* in the perfect and pluperfect tenses

Infinitive	Present	Imperfect	Perfect	English
beginnen	beginnt	begann	begonnen	to begin
bieten	bietet	bot	geboten	to offer
bleiben	bleibt	blieb	geblieben *	to stay
brechen	bricht	brach	gebrochen	to break
bringen	bringt	brachte	gebracht	to bring
denken	denkt	dachte	gedacht	to think
dürfen	darf	durfte	gedurft	to be allowed to
essen	isst	aß	gegessen	to eat
fahren	fährt	fuhr	gefahren *	to go, to travel
fallen	fällt	fiel	gefallen *	to fall
fangen	fängt	fing	gefangen	to catch
finden	findet	fand	gefunden	to find
fliegen	fliegt	flog	geflogen *	to fly
geben	gibt	gab	gegeben	to give
gehen	geht	ging	gegangen *	to go
genießen	genießt	genoss	genossen	to enjoy
gewinnen	gewinnt	gewann	gewonnen	to win
haben	hat	hatte	gehabt	to have
halten	hält	hielt	gehalten	to stop, to hold
hängen	hängt	hing	gehangen	to hang
helfen	hilft	half	geholfen	to help
kennen	kennt	kannte	gekannt	to know
kommen	kommt	kam	gekommen *	to come
können	kann	konnte	gekonnt	to be able to
lassen	lässt	ließ	gelassen	to leave, to allow
laufen	läuft	lief	gelaufen *	to run
leiden	leidet	litt	gelitten	to suffer
lesen	liest	las	gelesen	to read
liegen	liegt	lag	gelegen	to lie
mögen	mag	mochte	gemocht	to like
müssen	muss	musste	gemusst	to have to
nehmen	nimmt	nahm	genommen	to take

Infinitive	Present	Imperfect	Perfect	English
reiten	reitet	ritt	geritten	to ride
rennen	rennt	rannte	gerannt *	to run
rufen	ruft	rief	gerufen	to call
scheinen	scheint	schien	geschienen	to shine
schlafen	schläft	schlief	geschlafen	to sleep
schließen	schließt	schloss	geschlossen	to shut
schneiden	schneidet	schnitt	geschnitten	to cut
schreiben	schreibt	schrieb	geschrieben	to write
schwimmen	schwimmt	schwamm	geschwommen *	to swim
sehen	sieht	sah	gesehen	to see
sein	ist	war	gewesen *	to be
singen	singt	sang	gesungen	to sing
sitzen	sitzt	saß	gesessen	to sit
sollen	soll	sollte	gesollt	ought to
sprechen	spricht	sprach	gesprochen	to speak
stehen	steht	stand	gestanden	to stand
stehlen	stiehlt	stahl	gestohlen	to steal
steigen	steigt	stieg	gestiegen *	to climb
sterben	stirbt	starb	gestorben *	to die
tragen	trägt	trug	getragen	to carry, to wear
treffen	trifft	traf	getroffen	to meet
trinken	trinkt	trank	getrunken	to drink
tun	tut	tat	getan	to do
vergessen	vergisst	vergaß	vergessen	to forget
verlieren	verliert	verlor	verloren	to forget
waschen	wäscht	wusch	gewaschen	to wash
werden	wird	wurde	geworden *	to become
werfen	wirft	warf	geworfen	to throw
wissen	weiß	wusste	gewusst	to know
ziehen	zieht	zog	gezogen	to pull

Notes

Index of grammar topics

Thema 1 Ich persönlich
- A The present tense 3
- B Coordinating conjunctions 4
- C Plural nouns 4
- D Gender, case and definite and indefinite articles 5
- E Possessive adjectives 6
- F Quantifiers 6

Thema 2 Mein Zuhause
- A Adjectives 7
- B Adverbs 8
- C Prepositions with the dative case 8
- D Reflexive verbs 9
- E Separable verbs 10

Thema 3 Freizeit
- A Word order: inversion 11
- B Time, manner, place 11
- C Subordinating conjunctions 12
- D Expressing preferences 13

Thema 4 Die Schule
- A Negation and negative forms 15
- B Adverbs and adverbial phrases of time 15
- C Perfect tense: weak verbs 15
- D Perfect tense: irregular (strong) and mixed verbs ... 16
- E Perfect tense: verbs taking *sein* 16
- F Perfect tense: separable verbs 17

Thema 5 Berufe, Berufe…
- A Masculine and feminine job titles 18
- B Infinitive constructions: *um…zu* and *ohne…zu* 18
- C Infinitive constructions with and without *zu* 19
- D Cardinal numbers 20

Thema 6 …und in Zukunft?
- A Future tense 21
- B Adverbs and adverbial phrases for degree of certainty ... 22
- C Modes of address 22
- D Forming questions 23
- E Interrogative adjectives 23
- F Saying and writing German dates 24

Thema 7 Unterwegs
- A Imperative 25
- B *Zum/zur* 26
- C Modal verbs *können, wollen, sollen* 26
- D The genitive case (possession) 26

Thema 8 Ferien
- A Prepositions that always take the accusative 28
- B Prepositions that always take the dative 28
- C Prepositions taking either accusative or dative 29
- D Imperfect tense (of *sein, haben, es gibt*) 30

Thema 9 Gesundheit
- A Comparative adjectives and adverbs 31
- B Modal verbs *müssen* and *dürfen* 31
- C *Seit* and *schon* with present tense 32
- D Impersonal verbs with the dative 33
- E Dative reflexive pronouns 33
- F The passive voice 34

Thema 10 Meine Stadt und meine Gegend
- A Personal pronouns 35
- B The verb *gefallen* 36
- C Other verbs taking the dative 36
- D Indefinite pronouns 37

Thema 11 Einkaufen und so weiter
- A Asking questions using '*Was für…?*' 38
- B Forming questions using '*Welcher…?*' 38
- C Demonstrative adjectives and pronouns: *dieser* and *jener* ... 38
- D Relative pronouns 39

Thema 12 Essen und Trinken
- A Plural forms of nouns (revision) 41
- B Adjective endings in nominative/accusative (revision) ... 41
- C Using *gern/lieber/am liebsten* 42
- D The verb *schmecken* (revision) 42
- E Strong (irregular) verbs in the present tense 43
- F Subordinating conjunctions (revision): *damit, so dass, bevor, nachdem* ... 43

Thema 13 Medien
- A Imperfect tense 45
- B Pluperfect tense 45
- C Future tense (revision) 46
- D Summary of tenses 47
- E Adjectival endings after *etwas, nichts, viel, wenig, alles* ... 47

Thema 14 Die Umwelt
- A Impersonal verbs 49
- B The conditional 49
- C Comparative and superlative 51

Orders: please contact Bookpoint Ltd, 130 Milton Park, Abingdon, Oxon OX14 4SB. Telephone: (44) 01235 827827. Fax: (44) 01235 400401. Lines are open from 9.00 to 5.00, Monday to Saturday, with a 24-hour message answering service. You can also order through our website: www.hoddereducation.co.uk

If you have any comments to make about this, or any of our other titles, please send them to educationenquiries@hodder.co.uk

British Library Cataloguing in Publication Data

A catalogue record for this title is available from the British Library

ISBN 978 1 4718 3318 2

This edition published 2015.

Impression number 10 9 8 7 6 5 4 3

Year 2019, 2018, 2017, 2016

Copyright © 2015 Helen Kent and Marian Jones

All rights reserved. No part of this publication may be reproduced or transmitted in any form or by any means, electronic or mechanical, including photocopy, recording, or any information storage and retrieval system, without permission in writing from the publisher or under licence from the Copyright Licensing Agency Limited. Further details of such licences (for reprographic reproduction) may be obtained from the Copyright Licensing Agency Limited, of Saffron House, 6–10 Kirby Street, London EC1N 8TS.

Hachette UK's policy is to use papers that are natural, renewable and recyclable products and made from wood grown in sustainable forests. The logging and manufacturing processes are expected to conform to the environmental regulations of the country of origin.

Cover image is reproduced by permission of Fotolia.

Typeset in ITC Giovanni 9.5/12.5 pt by Aptara, Inc.

Printed in Great Britain for Hodder Education, an Hachette UK Company, Carmelite House, 50 Victoria Embankment, London EC4Y 0DZ

® IGCSE is the registered trademark of Cambridge International Examinations. This text has not been through the Cambridge endorsement process.